What is all the fuss about the New Age Movement?
What do satanists believe?
Do witches exist today?
Are there such things as ghosts?
What about demons?
Are psychics always bad news?
What's wrong with astrology?
Can a Christian ever become possessed?
Are all these movements contrary to God's Word?
How do we as Christians share the gospel in this New Age?
What steps should we take to protect our children?

Writing with expertise and in an easy-to-understand style, Dr. Nelson Price answers all of the above, plus many, many more of your questions about *New Age, the Occult and Lion Country.* He offers you a wealth of information—some so incredible you may think it unbelievable. Through interviewing New Age advocates, witches, warlocks and satanists, Dr. Price has gained inside knowledge of these movements. Eye-opening testimonies of people who have managed to escape from these false religions only serve to reinforce the dire need for Christians to combat the evils of the devil. It is vital for you, as a Christian, to be both knowledgeable about all diabolical beliefs and prepared to counteract them through your faith. The strategies provided in these pages will equip you to conquer the "roaring lion."

NEW AGE,
THE
OCCULT,
AND
LION COUNTRY

NELSON PRICE

NEW AGE,

THE

OCCULT,

AND

LION COUNTRY

Power Books

Fleming H. Revell Company
Old Tappan, New Jersey

Library of Congress Cataloging-in-Publication Data

Price, Nelson L.
  New age, the occult, and lion country / Nelson Price.
     p.   cm.
  Bibliography: p.
  ISBN 0-8007-5300-3
  1. New Age movement—Controversial literature. 2. Occultism— Controversial literature. 3. Devil. I. Title.
  BP605.N48P75   1989
  261.5'1—dc 19   89-3667
                                                                CIP

Copyright © 1989 by Nelson Price
Published by the Fleming H. Revell Company
Old Tappan, New Jersey 07675
Printed in the United States of America

CONTENTS

INTRODUCTION
THE ROARING
LION

"Be alert, be on watch! Your enemy, the Devil, roams around like a roaring lion, looking for someone to devour. Be firm in your faith and resist . . . ," the apostle Peter warned the early Christians (1 Peter 5:8, 9 TEV). No less than in ancient days does the lion roam the earth today; though he may wear another mask for twentieth-century America, he still prowls.

In ancient Egypt, Satan had his magicians; in Babylon, astrologers; in Assyria, dream manuals; in China the I Ching. Today he has mixed them all with a concoction of other occult arts in the caldron of our nation. Riots, rebellion, escalating crime rates, drug excesses, a flood of pornography in all the media give evidence that the lion still is "walking up and down in the earth" (*see* Job 1:7).

Such times are not days in which we need to be broadly open-minded. Instead we need enlightened and informed minds that will not allow admittance to all who knock. We need to ask ourselves, *Who is this on the doorstep?*

Even those skeptical about Satan's existence have become aware that something extraordinary is going on. Dan Sexton, a doctoral candidate in clinical psychology at the Professional School of Psychological Studies in Los Angeles, said, "We're not saying Satan's out there, but there are certain people out there who are human, acting on his behalf. There are people whose lives and jobs are secondary to their cult activities."[1] Reports of satanic crime have drastically increased, and across the country, police forces attempt to understand and deal with it.

A 60-percent increase—in one year!—of sales of *The Satanic Bible* and *Necronium*, commonly found in bookstores, evidences the increased popularity of the occult. In addition, the *Book of Shadows*, a diary in which practitioners record their cult-inspired activities, has shown remarkable sales increases.

We are living in lion country. Not only do we face the satanist, who advocates that God is basically evil and Satan a misunderstood ally of humankind, we come head to head with a diverse, sometimes baffling element that would tell us there is no one God, but that all is god and god is in everything. We call this element the New Age. Varied groups advocate the subtle nuances of the New Age occult consortium. Under the guise of motivational seminars, they have invaded government agencies and the business world, conducting "Full Potential Movement" seminars for such diverse groups as the IRS; CIA; the United States Army, Navy, and Air Force; NASA; GM; IBM; AT&T; Xerox; and BankAmerica. New Age music accounts for 30 percent of all sales in some music stores. To deal with either occult or New Age groups, born-again Christians need a proper view of the devil. He must be big enough, but not too big. In *The Screwtape Letters*, C. S. Lewis cautioned:

> There are two equal and opposite errors into which our race can fall about the devils: One is to disbelieve in their existence. The other is to believe, and feel an excessive and unhealthy interest in them. They, themselves, are equally pleased by both errors and hail a materialist or a medium with the same delight.[2]

Christians should not disregard the devil, calling belief in his existence impertinent and irrelevant, in view of our enlightened scientific progressiveness. Nor should they become preoccupied with the lion and his demonic cubs. Before reading anything on this subject, they need to pray. They will need to exert great mental and emotional self-discipline to withstand the blandishments of the devil. However, they can claim God's promise "greater is he that is in you, than he that is in the world" (1 John 4:4).

Though Satan *does* have power in this world, he is a wounded lion. By the shed blood of Jesus, he is forced to retreat. The Christian who rests in Him will be able to counteract the devil's works.

In the end, Revelation 20:1–3 (TEV) promises Satan's sure, eternal defeat: "Then I saw an angel coming down from heaven, holding in his hand the key of the abyss and a heavy chain. He seized the dragon, that ancient serpent—that is, the Devil, or Satan—and chained him up . . . [and] threw him into the abyss, locked it, and sealed it. . . ."

Having interviewed witches, warlocks, satanists, and New Age enthusiasts, I am convinced that in each instance Christianity faces a zealous group of devotees. To the numerous New Age advocates I have encountered, I want to say a special thanks. As a group they rank among the kindest and most gracious of persons. To them and all who read this book, I express my love and an invitation to join me in the joy inherent in Jesus Christ, who was conceived by the Holy Spirit in the virgin Mary—Emmanuel, God with us.

NEW AGE,

THE

OCCULT,

AND

LION COUNTRY

PART I
THE LION IN A NEW AGE

ONE

WHERE DO YOU FIND A NEW AGE?

At a New Age expo, a prominent lecturer told me, "Not all people are open to spiritual values, but they are open to success. So we invite them to success seminars and teach them spiritual values." Although the "spiritual values" they teach are basically pantheism and Hinduism, the New Age dresses them up in contemporary business terms, and most businesspersons don't know the difference.

The success-oriented business lecturer is on one end of the New Age spectrum. Close to the other end is Lea

Schultz of Lexington, Kentucky. Mrs. Schultz, who looks more down-to-earth than otherworldly, sits on a stool beneath a painting of the Last Supper. Brief announcements are made, including appeals for donations (a minimum of $15, please), and then the convener says it is time to "turn it over to Lea and Samuel."

Spritely Mrs. Schultz says, "It's great to see you, and I'm really glad you're here." Then she closes her eyes and softly says, "Bye." Her rate of respiration changes, her body wavers, and suddenly her head drops. A warm smile embraces her face as she slowly raises her head. When she opens her mouth, the voice of an alleged 700-year-old man named Samuel speaks with a Scottish brogue, "Well, greetings to you. . . ."

Lea Schultz is typical of "trance channelers" who claim to slip into trances and let extraterrestrials, age-old warriors, and their own "higher selves" speak through them. This vague but popular pseudoscientific spiritualism is what New Age adherents call "channeling."[1]

Whether you confront it in a business seminar or in a channeling session, there is no doubt that spiritual guerrilla warfare is being waged in America. This new assault has become so mixed and mingled with established values and institutions that it is hard to identify. Wheat and tares have never looked so much alike. We call it the New Age movement. Spelling *movement* with a little *m* hints at how undefined the effort is organizationally. It is not a cult, though there are cults within it. It is not a classic religion, though there are religious groups involved. Adherents draw what they think is best from many sources.

In contrast to orthodox Christianity, which accepts the Bible as its authoritative source, the New Age movement has no ultimate truth. It does not believe in a personal God who has the ultimate authority. Matter, truth, and being are held to be in a constant state of change. New revelation and rediscovered wisdom of the ages form the bases of their beliefs.

Previously, pagan spirituality was forced to the fringes of society and tabbed as "occult." Now, by using sophisticated terms and Western techniques, the occult connection often goes unnoticed. Regardless of its suave style, sophisticated speech, and contemporary representation, it is still the kingdom of darkness doing battle with the children of light.

As diverse as it is deceptive, the New Age movement encompasses a variety of organizations and individuals with similar religious perspectives. Many uninformed persons even contend that it is not occult in nature. However, it interprets Eastern religious concepts of pantheism (all is god, therefore you are god) for the West. It adopts Hindu polytheism and village religion to Western customs and language. It has become a sort of Protestant Hinduism, stripped of most of the Eastern gods of traditional Indian religion that would offend Western monotheism (the belief that there is one God).

The New Age movement in America emerged around 1971, when Eastern religious gurus and elitist mystical-occult teachers began to capitalize on a general spiritual disenchantment in the West.

A Personal Spiritual Path

Radical transformation of society is the ultimate objective of the movement. It begins on a personal level, with an awakening to a new reality of self. This is achieved by a form of universal energy that starts the person on a lifelong spiritual path known as a *sadhana*. Few can complete a sadhana in one lifetime. Through karma and reincarnation, this long-term progression may take several lifetimes.

Many in the movement base their faith on their understanding of cosmogony, that is, the theory of the genesis of the universe. To grasp their concept, picture a circle within a triangle. The circle represents the "Unmanifest Absolute," sometimes called God. The triangle represents impersonal forces known as *gunas*. These forces keep the Unmanifest Absolute under control. One guna lost control, and the restraining force was ruptured, which resulted in creation and a process called karma. This process of force going away from the Unmanifest Absolute is described by the word *sankhya*, which means "going away from." Ever since the rupture, humanity and all the forces of nature have been going away from their god nature. *Prodisankahya* means

18

"coming back to." Through karma and its twin fallacy called reincarnation, people are allegedly evolving back toward their god consciousness. According to this Hindu-based concept, everything evolves back to the ultimate, original Unmanifest Absolute. In this evolutionary process, our personalities are "blown away" or destroyed as we become conscious of our own god nature.

This nonbiblical system of works makes man responsible for God's error, the rupture. Human beings have to spend lifetimes locked in a vicious circle of trying to evolve back into becoming conscious that they are really god and are once more becoming the Unmanifest Absolute. It is totally foreign to all teaching of the Old and New Testaments. According to such thought, God does not reach us, but rather we reach God. Varied spin-offs of the theory exist. Rarely do inquirers or novices receive this teaching. No one asserts it in non–New Age forums.

Varied groups have made an effort to reach out to God through a New Age. A few years ago many New Agers even worked together to get things going on their own, to usher in the New Age.

Harmonic Convergence

Writer and artist Jose Arguelles, who taught at Evergreen State College, coined the term *harmonic convergence*. On August 16, 1987, New Age faithful the world over were to gather at sixty-three sacred "power points" to serve as a "human battery." The purpose was, in effect, to "jump start" a change in human consciousness. Everyone was to make a humming *om* sound to bring about this change. Publicly it was stated that this "om-ing" by a minimum of 144,000 persons would set in motion a change which by A.D. 2012 will enable humanity to harmonize with the energy of the earth, and peace will prevail.[2]

The date of this attempt to boost the world into a new age of harmony was allegedly set in accordance with the ancient Mayan calendar. Reputedly the ancient Mayan calendar had a great cycle beginning in 3113 B.C. and ending in A.D. 2012, when earthlings will again be in contact with aliens.[3]

Even if the principle had been plausible, the dates were not right. John B. Carlson, an astronomer and expert on the Mayan calendar said, "This has nothing whatsoever to do with rationality. It has to do with fun. Somebody will make a lot of money; there will be a lot of parties. . . ." He went on to say the Mayan calendar actually began in 3114 B.C. and was measured in cycles of less than twenty years rather than twenty-five, as the New Agers say.[4] Instead of being based on peace and love as alleged, the Mayan culture was actually based on violence, slavery, and blood sacrifices. Outside experts say the idea of harmonic convergence is a skyscraper of speculation built on scraps of science.

The day held more than met the public eye. It was actually a testing of the water to see if the world was ready for the emergence of "the Christ" of the New Age, an attempt to see how much public support New Ageism could gain. A similar attempt, called World Healing Day, had been made on December 31, 1986. The sponsoring Planetary Commission intended to reverse the "collective negative mass consciousness" to a "collective positive mass consciousness" by having millions of people worldwide pray (to whom, it didn't matter), meditate, and visualize peace.

Goals of a New Age

What do the New Agers look for? Within this broad spectrum of groups and people we'll find a searching mentality. You can see it in some of their buzzwords: *self-realization*, *self-awareness*, *illumination*, *enlightenment*, and *human potential*. The terms have their own appeal. However, anyone familiar with the Bible or human nature knows we have little "human potential" apart from Jesus Christ.

The Bible teaches we are fulfilled by loving God, accepting ourselves, and loving our neighbors. Persons attracted to New Age dogma spend thousands of dollars rejecting God, exploring themselves, and ignoring their neighbors. Adapting Hindu concepts, New Age advocates believe man is god and in him is the basic goodness needed for divinity. Lucifer was the original proponent of this when he said, "I will be like the most High" (Isaiah 14:14).

21

What Makes Up the New Age?

Christians may find the New Age difficult to understand because it crosses so many boundaries and appears to include groups that have little in common. A term used in the movement, *networking,* can help us understand its nature. Networks consist of autonomous units of people or organizations, which operate simultaneously as independent wholes and interdependent parts. It becomes nearly impossible to define where a network begins or ends. Most often one has no single center, headquarters, or dominant leader. This unity in diversity reflects New Age beliefs, principally *monism,* which is the world view that "all is one" and through enlightenment, a "new age" of peace and unity is dawning.

To understand how this network of diversity has impacted society, we'll look at the broad range of areas in which the New Age has influence:

> The spiritual realm
> Big business
> Healing

The Spiritual Realm

Some New Age influences relate to the spirit. As examples, we'll take a quick look at two related areas: channeling and crystals.

Channeling.   We've already met Lea Schultz, a "trance channeler." She is a living spiritualist who purportedly receives messages from someone now dead or who exists on a different plane or spiritual dimension. Christians might be most familiar with the idea from the Bible—when King Saul visited the witch of En-dor, he became involved in the same practice, when the witch acted as a medium. A channeler has a different name but does the same thing

Essentially, this occult process presumes to use esoteric information to acquire supernatural spiritual powers. The channel allegedly goes into an altered state of consciousness and allows "someone else" to use his or her body and voice to speak to people presently living. The "force" using the channel is known by a variety of titles, some of which are: *spirit guides god, higher being discarnate spirit*, or *disembodied spirit* Channels reputedly have supernatural sensitivity, which enables them to receive high-pitched frequencies from the spirit world.

Another current popular channel, J. Z. Knight, represents herself as frequently being contacted by a being called Ramtha. The public is often admitted to "interviews" with Ramtha for a charge of between $150 and $350 per person.

Some less dramatic forms of channeling involve visualization, mantras, meditation, crystals, out-of-body experiences, tarot cards, and sound and light experiences. Channels tend to avoid consulting with the dead, though they have no reluctance about contacting higher spirit teachers. Such a contact may be known as the great white brotherhood, an ascended master, or the medium's own higher self.

From Manhattan to Malibu this bizarre procedure gains momentum. The number of professional channels in California alone exceeds 1,000. Peter Sanders, director of Free Soul, a psychic-training program based in Arizona, claims 25,000 students.

Not all New Age groups engage in channeling. Some don't even know about it. Many who engage in the milder forms do not realize what it is. This further indicates the broad variety of views and practices in the movement.

Crystal Clear. *Forbes* magazine reports that the public buys $100 million worth of crystals a year and anticipates the market will grow to $250 million worldwide within five years.[5] Devotees believe that by using crystals they can amplify positive thoughts, remove mental blocks, achieve inner balance, increase personal awareness, and cure physical illnesses.

Advocates say crystals link ancient metaphysical beliefs by the Mayans, Tibetans, Incans, and American Indians with the current emphasis on self-help, inner healing, and interplanetary responsibility.

"Crystal technologists" advise people that everyone has God's spark within. To fan it a little brighter, they say, a person must be brushed with crystal healing. Those involved in "crystal consciousness" will use quartz crystals and their colorful relatives, amethyst, citrine, smoky, and rose quartz, seeking to bring about such change.

Although scientists will agree that crystals have certain properties, among them a piezoelectric effect, which means they produce a minute electric charge when compressed, simple squeezing by hand will not provide detectable levels of change in energy or "charge."

Highly skeptical, most scientists believe crystals produce nothing more than a placebo effect. George Harlow, curator of gems and minerals at the American Museum of Natural History, is quoted in *Omni* magazine as saying, "All this baloney only proves that we have failed, and failed miserably, in teaching of science. There is simply no evidence that there is any measurable effect from crystal to human, or any kind of healing."[6]

Crystal users assume that if quartz can be programmed in timepieces or computers, it can be programmed mentally to conduct or amplify the electric currents in their bodies. Proponents say the human makeup consists of crystals. Even our brain cells are crystals, and stones balance the body with positive cosmic energy.[7]

Devotees are urged to chant their intention into a crystal and to pray through it. They think of it as being so personal that Dolfyn, a crystal technologist, said, "In an alienated society like this one, if you need a friend, you've got one in a crystal."[8] Benefits claimed from crystals include health, self-healing, emotional balancing, obtaining wealth, channeling energy, and divination for diagnosis or finding answers to issues.

New Age Business

Although the New Age movement is unorganized, has no dogma, and tends to shun publicity,[9] it has spawned magazines, newspapers, bookstores, a music industry, and seminars for business professions. A local "Holistic Resource Directory" lists 400 churches, businesses, bookstores, counselors, and teachers.

Newsweek reported that Pacific Bell, Procter & Gamble, Ford Motor Company, and Polaroid have signed New Age consultants to help employees "get in touch" with the god within. RCA, Scott Paper, and Boeing have secured the services of Transformational Technologies, a firm that helps companies become "metanoic ' A major telephone company plans to pass on to its customers the $147 million cost of New Age training for its employees.[10]

Forbes reported that over $300 million worth of audio and videotapes were sold in a single year, demonstrating "ways of harnessing the power of the mind to influence the body."[11] Some bookstores estimate that 30 percent of their sales are of New Age materials.[12]

New Age philosophy and techniques have made dramatic inroads into the business community under clever disguises. This was done by proposing increased sales, better workman performance, and improved health.

Carl Raschke, a University of Denver humanities professor, commented, "Motivational psychology has been a key dimension of business training programs for the last century." What is different, he says, "is the New Age thinking as a synthetic kind of religion using various forms of behavioral psychology and thought modification."[13]

The spiritual phase of the New Age movement involves mediums, reincarnation, the occult, psychic healing, satanism, and new metaphysical religions. However, the business community seeks to take advantage of another completely different, yet associated phase, often referred to as the "human potential" movement. By incorporating spiritual concepts from Asian religions, those who teach this method profess to transform clients into more creative and productive members of the work force. In doing so they never allude to any of their methods or materials as having roots in the East.

Programs infected with New Age thinking include Lifespring, D.M.A., Silva Mind Control, World Institute of Scientological Enterprises (WISE), Movement of Inner Spiritual Awareness (MISA), Insight Personal Seminars, Managing Accelerated Productivity (MAP), and Actualizations. For a program to be effective, a person must adopt the new view (often called paradigm shift) that underlines the change being sought. The results are increased acceptance of reincarnation, karma, monism (or pantheism), synchronicity (the belief of the interconnectedness of all life), cosmic unity, paranormal phenomena, and out-of-body experiences.[14]

The Sound of a New Age. The New Age does not just influence big business; in the music industry, it *is* big business. Perhaps it also exerts no more subtle influence than it does with music. New Age music, mostly instrumental, aims at the subconscious mind and is programmed to affect levels of consciousness. Nicknamed *audio Valium*, in some markets, New Age records and tapes now account for as much as 30 percent of sales. Producers of this new type of sound waves rush to deny that there is anything hypnotic about their music, but they advertise that these designer sound waves "soften and reverse your stubborn subconscious."

Musician Suzanne Ciani has created music that she describes as "very personal. . . . It really springs up from this deep reservoir of Jungian dreamlike emotions." The music is intended to reach the subconscious mind through sounds that are inaudible to the brain's conscious hearing. They are, however, clear and impressionable to the subconscious mind.[15]

As with all things, how the music is used is of importance. Proponents boast it brings deep rest, additional energy and strength, disappearance of anxiety and worry, and hallucination of bright colors, symbols, lights, and faces, passing before them in a magnificent parade. Professional psychics admit they use the cassettes to increase their psychic abilities.

We must evaluate New Age music in light of the overall movement and its objectives. Some of the music has a positive message, but much of this front music serves as an entree for more subtle New Age teachings.

Proponents profess the innocence of New Age music, but the warning on some record jackets—DO NOT LISTEN TO THIS WHILE DRIVING—reveals its danger. Because the music results in an altered state of consciousness, it not only presents a danger when one drives, it also makes one open to demonic intrusion. When a person becomes vulnerable to all forces, the subconscious can be invaded by occult powers—and he or she can remain unaware of what has occurred.

Healing in a New Age

Not only does the New Age influence the spiritual and business realms, it has an impact on physical and psychological areas, too.

A woman suffers from repeated migraine headaches, but distrusts the medical profession. When a friend tells her about biofeedback, which promises to rid her of the headaches without any medication at all, she decides to try it. Before long she experiences relief from the headaches—and has begun to use it to develop psychic abilities she never knew she had. The therapist she went to belonged to the New Age movement, and now she does, too.

A journalist visits China and suffers from appendicitis. After the operation, he is treated for gastritis by an acupuncturist. Soon his experiences become a praise-filled article in the *New York Times*.[16]

In an age of deteriorating ecology, a sedentary life-style that brings on physical problems and increases in diseases such as cancer, heart attacks, and stress-related difficulties, people have begun to look beyond conventional medical technology. Dissatisfied with the American medical system, which they perceive as ineffective and uncaring, many patients have turned to the New Age for answers. Perhaps this accounts for new or renewed interest in the medical values of procedures such as:

> *Biofeedback*, which uses electronic equipment to control brain waves that influence bodily function and may result in a search for other levels of consciousness.
>
> *Hypnosis*, which seeks to release healing energy from within the mind.
>
> *Yoga*, a system of physical exercise with a little more to it than most people expect, since it has a basis in Hinduism.
>
> *Acupuncture and acupressure*, two methods of pain reduction that seek to redirect the "life forces," based on Taoist philosophies.
>
> *Homeopathy*, a theory propounded by Samuel Hahnemann, which claims that "like cures like" and prescribes diluted substances that cause a symptom in a healthy body to heal the ill one.
>
> *Psychic healing*, as practiced by someone who seeks to make use of energy fields or occult powers.[17]

All New Age technologies see man's health solution as lying in energy. Whether they call it Ch'i, prana, vital energy, or something else, they speak of the same New Age concept. New Agers see energy as the common denominator in all life, and seek to manipulate it for health. Healers attempt to channel energy within the body to remove blocks—and "heal."

Benefits and Drawbacks of the New Age Outlook. Granted, the New Age has had some positive influences upon medicine:

> It has brought to the fore our need to treat the body, mind, and spirit together. Traditional medicine *had* become so specific it sometimes forgot that understanding one ·part of this triad might not be enough.
> It has advocated positive wellness, not just negative illness. Perhaps today's focus on exercise, which has increased in the past twenty years, has been influenced· by New Age ideas.
> It has actively sought to have people become part of their own health care. By not accepting medical technologies, New Agers made people more aware of the limitations of medicine.

But these by-products do not tell the whole story. New Age concepts have not improved medicine when they have advocated a basically nonscientific approach that encourages the use of systems long ago disproved.

By encouraging people to accept anything that differs

from traditional medicine, they have often opened the door to more problems. Those who do not carefully check out these claims may find themselves more abused by would-be healers than they were by practitioners of conventional medicine.

Prior to taking part in such methods, people need to ask:

> *What does the practitioner promise?*
> Raising expectations that cannot be fulfilled may lead desperate people to follow a technique, but will those promises be kept?
> *What are the proven results?*
> Are unbiased statistics available? Has the "cure" lasted? A multitude of personal testimonials will not suffice. What are the hard facts?
> *Is the practitioner open about results?*
> A secretive attitude may indicate he or she has something to hide.
> *What does the medical community say about the results?*
> Despite the stories about the excesses of conventional medicine, such a system may do less to harm people than some who attack the medical establishment. Anyone seeking healing should beware of frauds.

In addition, Christians will want to avoid anything that has a New Age or occult background.

Mental Health in a New Age. Mentally the New Age has a goal: self-realization. Because it sees man as god, it seeks to make the most of him by bringing him to his highest powers. To do so, it encourages him to seek divine oneness and to "change his reality."

Those who have turned to the New Age may have felt the pressures of a modern age. Isolated in a large society that deifies individualism, they may now seek to understand their larger world through the transformation promised by the New Age. Focusing on innate abilities may seem a shortcut to healthy self-esteem, but the New Ager may actually discover more problems than he solves.

Many in the New Age will not so suspend reality that it causes them intense psychological problems. For the borderline or psychotic individual, however, the psychology of the New Age can prove dangerous.[18] The burden it places upon a tenuous self-esteem may prove overwhelming.

Common Ground?

What do all these diverse elements have in common? New Age groups share five teachings:

1. The essential concept that "all is one." This is called monism, from the Greek root meaning "one."
2. The teaching that "all is god." Such thought, based on ancient pantheism, abandons the Christian view of a personal God in favor of an impersonal energy, force, or consciousness.
3. The claim "we are all god, whether or not we realize

it." Actress Shirley MacLaine said her spirit guide informed her, "If everyone was taught one basic spiritual law, your world would be a happier, healthier place. And that law is this: Everyone is God. Everyone."[19]

4. The belief that a "consciousness awakening," a new way of interpreting the events of life, is needed. Eastern meditation, yoga, martial arts, hypnosis, or drugs can aid this.

5. Such a revolution of consciousness leads to spiritual power as a person realizes his or her human potential.

In a single statement, the New Age movement teaches that as self-realized gods, we inherit the supernatural. As lords of our own universe, we create our own reality by the power of our thoughts. The New Age violates God's will because it advocates worshiping the creature rather than the Creator (Romans 1:25).

You Call This a Conspiracy?

Is the New Age movement a conspiracy intent on taking over the world? No and yes.

From a human vantage point, the answer appears to be no. However, if it *is* one, it is not a very well organized conspiracy. Some networks *are* close-knit and insidious, relentlessly pursuing social, economic, and political goals that would revolutionize America. Like all movements the New Age does have militants, who desire radical change.

The goals of the radical end of the New Age movement are personal power and a global utopia. To achieve this, they would replace the Western world view, including Christianity, with a "new planetary consciousness." The *Networking Book* lists 1,526 organizations that share this resolve to "build another America."[20]

If the New Age has a unifying point and person, it would appear to be Shirley MacLaine. The primary popular exponent of the movement, she plans to build a spiritual center in Colorado. Another center is the Palo Alto Creative Initiative Foundation, a think tank in California. If the movement has a bible, it would be Marilyn Ferguson's *The Aquarian Conspiracy*.[21] But basically the New Age has become so organizationally diverse that one can hardly see it as an effective political or social conspiracy. The overwhelming number of individuals and groups involved in the New Age who do not have a commitment to taking over the world makes the others look a lot less threatening. Often the bulk of New Age groups do not even appear to know the agenda of the more radical elements.

From a supernatural vantage point, however, we might call the New Age an emerging conspiracy. Its devaluation of Jehovah God; Jesus Christ, who was born of Mary in Bethlehem; and the Holy Spirit, sent by

Christ, has to be satanic. Mere mortals could never have devised something this clever. In part Christ described the satanic conspiracy when He said, ". . . many shall come in my name, saying, I am Christ; and shall deceive many" (Matthew 24:5).

TWO

VISIT TO
THE NEW AGE

Recently, on a visit to a New Age expo, I chatted with exhibitors to learn firsthand how they viewed the movement. Some were merely fairly innocent entrepreneurs providing services and products for the New Age community. They exhibited such things as water purification systems, computers, food supplements, clothing, tests for radon gas, air filtration systems, and exercise programs.

Another group, which I put in a gray area, provided a service not necessarily part of the New Age movement, but often associated with it. Among them were exhibitors involved with chiropractic, massage therapy, and associated arts.

A third group consisted of obviously occult arts, practices, and materials Visit them with me as I stop at some of the booths.

Behind her display of crystals, Carol, a striking brunette, claims, "You make your own reality."

At another booth, "Keepers of the Flame" tell us about Saint Germain. They affirm he is the patron of the United States of America and hierarch of the Aquarian age. Along with the goddess Liberty, the Divine Mother God, whose statue they believe stands in New York Harbor, Saint Germain is guardian of "the Flame." In a golden age, more than fifty thousand years ago, they tell us, he sealed knowledge in the hearts of Lightbearers who had served with him in a fertile land where the Sahara Desert is now. These once mighty people have been reincarnated on American soil, called by Saint Germain from many nations to return to the Law of the One.

According to the Keepers of the Flame, in the heart of every person burns a one-sixteenth-of-an-inch triparted blue, yellow, and pink flame, representing the trinity. Blue speaks of the Father principle, to be worshiped as God the Lawgiver. Yellow represents Christos, the eternal Son, the teacher who taught wisdom. Pink depicts the Holy Spirit, who ministers love. The white core at the heart represents the Divine Mother.[1]

As we move to the next booth, we meet "Bartholomew," who speaks through Mary Margaret Moore, of Albuquerque, New Mexico. Bartholomew was first manifested on our plane of consciousness on December 3, 1977. In a state of hypnosis (an art broadly used in the New Age), Mrs. Moore had this outside energy or intelligence speak through her. Asked to name the greatest of the way showers, Bartholomew named Krishna, the Buddha, Christ, Shankaracharya, and Ramana.

A little farther on, we meet a New Age enthusiast named Emmanuel, who has defined *heaven* as "the space within each one of you that dances in the light."

A visit with Crazy Owl, a Californian who has come to tell people how to avoid AIDS, will give us insight into "the third eye." Confidently he explains the seventy-four meridians of the body through which energy can be lost or gained. These are also healing and enlightenment points. To gain energy or insight, one must place specific stones on given parts of the anatomy. Placement of a fluorite stone on the forehead opens the third eye. Through this meridian, energy and insight enter through the pineal gland. Thus the third eye allegedly sees what ordinary people can't. Reputedly this process opens spiritual understanding.

As we move along, we come to a booth promoting acupressure, part of the healing practices of the Taoist religion. It is commonly called "traditional Chinese medicine." Proponents have learned to use 43 of the 364 acupoints and to affect ch'i energy flows in the eight ancestral channels or strange flows. Sometimes people call this "acupuncture with your fingers." Advanced students learn foot reflexology, hand reflexology, aura balancing, ear massage, and Taoist medical exercises.

A stop at the Avatar Perception Training display shows us how the New Age groups communicate subtle pantheism and basic Hindu philosophy through business seminars. As its theme, this exhibit has taken the concept "beliefs provide your experiences." "From random thought, belief is formed, thus the experience occurs to prove the belief true. Such is the simplicity of it all," they inform us.

Perception training professes to provide the tools for dismantling realities and states of self one no longer wishes to experience. It begins with opening a perception channel to the physical universe. Students learn to create a reality at will; this produces a state called "clear" or "enlightenment." In a third exercise, a student learns to suspend judgments of any thing or event in life. Thus begins the quick erosion of lifelong convictions and the embracing of pantheistic concepts.

At the iridology booth, we discover a school of thought that begins with a scriptural truth: "The light of the body is the eye: if therefore thine eye be single, thy whole body shall be full of light" (Matthew 6:22). From there iridology dramatically departs from the Bible. It represents itself as providing the "tools" necessary for humans to understand who they are and what is necessary for growth on the evolutionary path. The left eye, iridologists maintain, displays issues with creativity, right-brain functions, and feminine maturity (Mom). The right eye displays issues with logic, left-brain activities, and masculine relationships (Dad). Seed thoughts displayed in the iris and sclera are linked, through the subconscious, to a person's life situation. A trained iridologist claims to read these conditions and help that person up-scale his or her life and emotions.

Rembrandt, Vincent Van Gogh, Amedeo Modigliani, Toulouse-Lautrec, and others are back at our next stop. They now all paint through Luiz Gasparetto, Brazilian gestalt psychologist and psychic medium. In a style he acknowledges is similar to former great artists, the psychic paints in the dark, while in a trance, or in a lighted room, with his eyes closed. As if that were not enough, he becomes mysteriously ambidextrous. He may paint with both hands at once, sometimes doing a third painting with his feet. Channeling one artist through his right arm and another through his left, he may also achieve a third style through his feet. It all happens quickly and simultaneously.

At the expo numerous forms of Yoga purport to solve everything imaginable. Proponents sell Yoga to the

American public as a means of increasing energy, feeling better, and developing better health. Many instructors sincerely believe that is all they are doing. Actually they cultivate a state of mind and moral code compatible with Hinduism. While a naive person goes through Yoga exercises thinking he or she simply gets exercise, a true exponent knows the process is designed "to move the serpent force up the spine to the brain." Often this occult practice is accompanied by a repeated mantra, intended to develop a higher state of consciousness. By repeating the mantra, the person invocates a Hindu god.

Yoga, which means "to yoke," was not devised as a physical exercise program, but as a religious rite. Hatha Yoga, represented as simply exercise, has as its purpose yoking with the Hindu god Brahma.

An advanced Yoga instructor describes the connection between the spiritual and Yoga: "There is no Yoga without Hinduism. Yoga is the highest form of Hinduism, the very heart. The hope of immortality is Yoga."

The Bhagavad Gita says Yoga is the way out of the reincarnation cycle. Western minds may think of reincarnation as a form of mysticism, but a true Hindu knows it is a form of punishment for not having reached true god consciousness.

How subtly Yoga works its way into our society! We can see this in the December, 1984, issue of *Boy's Magazine*, a publication for Boy Scouts. An article entitled "What Is Yoga?" states: "Yoga is a set of ancient poses and exercises that strengthen the muscles, strengthen the body, and discipline the mind." The author encourages its practice: ". . . You will find it a good tool for whatever challenges—mental or physical—come along."[2]

As we continue in the expo, we listen to a proponent of macrobiotics, who tells of the benefits of being a vegetarian. "When meat is consumed, it drags the soul downward. Vegetation pulls up the soul. Persons outside the movement are evil because they are flesh eaters."

No New Age expo would be complete without a stop at the Transcendental Meditation booth. In the West, Maharishi Mahesh Yogi popularized TM, also called "the Science of Creative Intelligence."

Introductory lecturers present charts and graphs that represent TM as a scientifically verified mental technique for gaining deep rest and insights, including a boundless potential for creativity and the release of wisdom, which reputedly lies within each of us. To the uninformed, it is presented as a simple technique for obtaining such benefits. Those initiated into the movement learn it is also a technique for gaining spiritual goals.

The roots of TM lie in the important Hindu scripture, the Bhagavad Gita. In his commentary on it, the Maharishi explains why TM is presented as one thing to nonmeditators and another to those who have begun it: "If the enlightened man wants to bless one who is ignorant, he should . . . try to lift him up from there by giving him the key to transcending [that is, TM], so that he may gain bliss-consciousness and experience the Reality of Life. He should not tell him about the level of the realized because it would only confuse him."[3] This primary, unstated goal is to permanently alter the meditator's perception of the world until it harmonizes with the Hindu pantheistic worldview.

TM's initially successful attempts to market itself as "secular" received a major setback when, in 1976, a United States federal court legally identified it as "religion." This ruling was upheld, on appeal, in 1979.

At a conference on TM in India, in 1981, a spokesman for the movement revealed its undercurrent of hostility toward Christianity by saying, "The entire mission of TM is to counter the ever spreading demon of Christianity."[4] Many naive practitioners of TM do not perceive this objective of the movement, which to them advocates nothing more than deep rest and creativity. They do not understand that the *creative* part mentioned in the literature means remolding the mind to conform to pantheism.

As our last stop at the expo, we visit a prominent proponent of the New Age, named Lazaris. "At one time spirituality was seated in Tibet, in the Himalayan Mountains," he tells us. "That is where many seekers went, ultimately, to find the various teachings and wisdoms and secrets—that sort of thing. Perhaps that was the case, but now the seat of spirituality has moved. It is now in the United States."[5]

Ira Friedlander, an early sympathetic observer, described the same phenomenon this way:

> Great spiritual energy has been moved to this country, and holy men of the East are following it, and, of course, they bring the Light within them to become mirrors. They establish "ashrams" and reconfirm the spiritual centers within ourselves. They plant the seeds of inner peace with their divine grace, which remains and nourishes like a good rain that falls on fertile soil; long after the rain has gone, the seed in the soil continues to grow.[6]

In the early days, some Christian authors used overstatements and exaggerated interpretations, causing some people to disregard their warnings concerning the New Age. Now one could hardly overstate the case, but we still need insight and education to counteract the movement. Those who doubted the claim that a lion lay in the brush need wonder no longer, but unfortunately, the lion still looks a lot like a lamb.

Sometimes we become like little Max, a child known for his active imagination. One day he ran into the house, screaming, "There is a lion in our yard! Help."

His understanding dad caught him and said, "Son, you know there is no lion in our yard."

"Yes, there is a big lion on our sidewalk," insisted the child.

To reassure Max and teach him a lesson about lying, Dad walked him out into the yard. There they found what Max reported to be a lion—Lady, the neighbors' new collie.

Back in the house, Dad insisted Max go to his room and pray about lying, until he knew God had forgiven him. A short time later Max came downstairs.

"Did you ask God to forgive you?" Dad asked.

Happily Max replied that he had.

"What did God say?"

With a big smile, Max responded, "God said the first time He saw that dog, He thought it was a lion, too."

Max thought the dog was a lion, but as we have fallen for New Age deceptions, we have believed the lion was a lamb. The first time we encounter them, such ideas may seem harmless enough. But we must remember that what New Age groups show to the uninitiated is often far different from what lies behind this innocent facade. By merging legitimate and quasi-legitimate elements, New Age groups have kept their true nature hidden.

The word *occult* means "hidden, concealed, secret, revealed only to the initiated." Though many people have never thought of the New Age in these terms, if they can accept this common dictionary definition of the word, see what the movement hides, and realize that it often uses the means of more "conventional" occult groups, they *will* define the New Age movement as occult.

One thing we'll find hidden behind the face of the changeable lion, is a common view of reality. Though diverse in its expression, this concept repeatedly surfaces in New Age groups.

THREE
FINDING A PLACE IN REALITY

Channeled by Lea Schultz, Samuel teaches that Jesus Christ, as a Piscean teacher, ascended out of the grave into a new life, not into heaven. Ascension, according to Samuel, occurs when body and mind, in response to the spirit, make a total change and an enlightened self comes about, physically, chemically, mentally, and spiritually.[1]

Winsome young Gary Bonnelle, who teaches classes on ascension and astral projection at the Ascension Principle Center, based in Atlanta, teaches that ascen-

49

sion is the next jump for mankind, a quantum leap. What is his authority for such a statement? He says, "When I walked with Jesus, as the Apostle James, he instructed that Ascension is something that will happen to those who desire it."[2]

Bonnelle believes that in order to experience ascension, one must only drop control, self-righteousness, and the need to be right. When he dropped the need to be right, he alleges he in essence became the Christ vibration and automatically ascended. Therein he discovered his Christ being.[3]

In his class, he explains the process this way:

> The way Ascension works is by changing the vibrational field of the body through *knowing* that you are the center, knowing that nothing outside you exists, period, save for the fact that you wanted it to be there, knowing that your kingdom is not of this world. When Christ was asked by Pilate why did he not defend himself, Christ said, "the only power you have over me is the power I give to you," and "my kingdom is not of this world." What he was trying to express is that this world is a wonderful place to play and that I am here in it, but I am not of it.[4]

Margaret and Andris Priede document and communicate the process of going from "the human condition to the divine state of being." They assert that at this time in evolution, ascension by millions is possible. Countless individuals before us have done it, they maintain. Ascension means the process of becoming one with God; when this happens, fear, doubt, ignorance, intolerance, degeneration, disease, and death will no longer influence us. To achieve this, one must align the dense body with its ethereal counterpart, without physical death. The Priedes believe the New Age is all about the completion of the human cycle of experience and the divine state of being.[5]

Karen Glueck channels Father Andre, an entity who alleges to have ascended during his last incarnation. He teaches: "Ascension happens when the body and the soul merge through the heart and all limitations fall off. . . . It is a visual, physical expression of ascension."[6]

Confronted with so many differing concepts of the same word, all flying beneath the banner of the New Age, no wonder Christians feel confusion. Add to that the New Age tendency to take Christian words and redefine them, and it seems less surprising that Christians confronted with familiar words often think they face a lamb, not a lion. But the lion does not have his basis in mainline Christianity, no matter what terms he uses.

All New Age groups come from a common school of thought that has its roots in Hinduism, with a smattering of Buddhism, Taoism, and Confucianism thrown in. It even has links with shamanism, animism, and spiritism. Though they may never use these terms, in some form or another, New Age adherents espouse the philosophies they describe.

The Reality of the New Age

Perhaps the most popular catchphrase of the New Age is "You make your own reality." Most groups in the movement offer a confusing combination of nirvana and utopia, but all base their principles on the search for self-gratification and self-fulfillment.

What is this reality they advocate? Let's consider some of its teachings and inconsistencies.

Karma and Reincarnation

Karma, Hinduism's sort of spiritual accounting system, says that everything balances out and that all persons have earned their present state as a result of actions in their past lives. For example, if a property owner imposes on tenants in this life, the law of karma, which demands retribution, will cause him to come back in another life (through reincarnation) as a tenant to be abused.

Reincarnationists believe that when the "karmic debt" is balanced, the soul returns to the "Source," sometimes called God or the Cosmic Consciousness. Therefore, if you see a person suffering or grieving, you should not try to help him. By doing so you would disrupt the law of karma and cause him to come back in another life, to receive his punishment.

To those in the New Age, abortion is related to reincarnation. The aborted fetus simply has his or her reentry into personhood rescheduled. In the meantime, the soul simply waits in some other state for its readmission into the human family. New Agers envision the preborn spirit of the unwanted or undesirable conception saying things such as:

"I want the best deal I can get. I'll wait, thank you."
"I'll gladly wait for the right time and circumstances."
"Take your time. There is no rush. I have all the time in the world."

To the New Age, being pro-life means you want a child to be born only under the best of circumstances.

But the concept of improving a person's place conflicts with the ideology of karma, which claims that one's life results from circumstances in a previous life. Under this belief putting off births could not result in better circumstances. Aborting a child would merely frustrate his or her karma.

Under karma and reincarnation, how long can compassion last in a society? And if karma dictates what we have coming, how can we make our own reality, as the New Age groups claim?

Your Reality and Everybody Else's Mess

I made a note when I heard the engaging New Age lecturer say, "When you give up the need to always be right, you then discover that everybody else is right." During a question-and-answer time, he added, "When your life is right, when it is centered, then you can begin to help other people out of the mess they are in."

How can others be in a mess if they are always right? I wondered.

Further complicating the issue, the speaker went on, "By dropping the need to be in control, the need to be right, you in essence become the 'right.' "

This comfortable "me right" world would soon come in conflict with that of others, who are right by their standards. Since everybody will not have the same ideas, somebody is obviously wrong. If anything, I'd say it's the theory we started with.

Nature and High-Tech Realities

On one hand natural things such as macrobiotics, acupressure, acupuncture, massage therapy, crystals, and primitive physical foods and methods are represented as the path of the New Age. Many institutions thrive by selling such products or teaching these techniques.

On the other hand, New Age expos have a proliferation of plastic and high-tech equipment. Transcendental Meditation, now thought to be too time consuming, has a rival in a machine called a Synchro-Energizer. It costs $50,000 and alleges to speed up the process. One Synchro-Energizer salesman described his product by saying, "We're selling Buddha in a can."[7]

Using a technique called "mindwalking," which results in an altered state, clinics with names such as *Tranquility Center*, *Altered States*, and *Universe of You* offer to achieve in fifteen minutes what formerly required ten years of Yoga instruction. These "mind gyms" offer $300 memberships.

In a mindwalking session, students put on headphones and goggles with four lights around each eye. Through the headphones they hear the sound of a heartbeat, assorted clicks, then a sound like a lawn sprinkler. This fades into synthesized music, accompanied by the sound of pounding surf. In one clinic, after a session, patrons are invited into an adjoining room, where an orange statue of Buddha, wearing Walkman headphones, confronts them.

Dr. Stephen Peroutka, an assistant professor in the neurology department at Stanford University, remarked regarding the process: "If flashing lights and goggles help you relax, that's good. Relaxation is always good for the body." However, he concluded, "There is no scientific evidence that any mechanical device can enhance learning or creativity. . . . There's no magic way to do it."[8]

God's Place in Reality

If we push the New Age concept that we can create our own reality to its farthest point, it means nothing happens to us that we don't desire and allow. One can hardly imagine that all the nearly 6 million Jews killed in the holocaust wanted that to happen. If humans are gods, we have made an awful mess of things.

The concept of making our own reality perverts a vital principle: We can't determine what happens to us, but we *can* choose how to react. By saying we will into being all that happens to us, the New Age disallows natural circumstances or the influence of other persons. It also is tantamount to denying the existence of any supernatural power greater than the will of man, precluding the existence of God and Satan. The basic fallacy of the movement can be summed up in its belief that each of us is his or her own universe.

Like the man in Isaiah 44, who cut down cedar trees and used the wood for various purposes, making a god of the residue, the New Age has made its own gods—men.

Not only does the New Age defy God's warnings against such idolatry, the movement as a whole is anti-Bible. Many of its devotees may quote Scripture, but they also seek to redefine it. Unlike early twentieth-century German and American theologians who tried to "demythologize" the Bible, New Age proponents have overmythologized Scripture. They take historical and factual events and turn them into symbols and myths.

The New Age has many theological differences with Christianity, but it begins with their differences on how they view God.

Basically, we can see God in one of three ways:

    Diversity
    Diversity in unity
    Unity

Which we choose decides what kind of God we have.

Diversity

This view says Jehovah is one of many gods.

Mankind has always tended to create gods, and as Romans 1:23 describes, can come up with a wide variety of homemade gods: ghoulish ones, hybrids of men and animals, or as the Greeks did, gods like men. By fashioning gods to meet their desires and needs, men ended up with less-demanding deities than Jehovah—but with awful results (Romans 1:26–32).

Part of Satan's lie to Adam and Eve was that if they disobeyed God and ate the forbidden fruit they would become gods. New Agers quote this text as "proof" that we are literally gods. Remember, though, when Satan first used that line, it was a lie—and it hasn't changed since.

Diversity in Unity

According to this view, only one God exists, but we know Him by many names and means. Those who believe in diversity in unity say Jehovah, Allah, Buddha, and so on are all the same. Many New Age personnel hold this view.

The Bible has many passages asserting that only one God exists, and He is named Jehovah. The rest of the gods also have characteristics unbecoming to His nature as revealed in Scripture.

Unity

The final concept says there is only one God. Scripture defines this part of His nature in many passages including:

> ". . . The Lord our God is one Lord" (Deuteronomy 6:4).
> ". . . I the Lord thy God am a jealous God . . ." (Exodus 20:5).
> "You believe that there is one God. You do well . . ." (James 2:19 NKJV).

Christian unity also says God can only be known in one way, through Jesus Christ, who was born in Bethlehem. John 3:16 says "For God so loved the world, that he gave his only begotten Son. . . ." "Only begotten" is a translation of the Greek *monogenes*. In that language, *mono* means "one," and *genes* means "kind or type." Those who claim we are all sons of God just like Jesus don't understand that this teaches He was God's only, one-of-a-kind Son.

Nor is Christ any less than the Father. When Scripture calls Jesus the Son of God, it does not speak of generation. A good, unabridged dictionary defines *son* as "one closely associated with a nation, race, or belief." This term speaks of association. Christ has a coequal association with the Father and Spirit. All three parties of the Godhead have one will. Paul clearly identified Jesus and noted that He was fully God: "In Him dwells all the fullness of the Godhead bodily" (Colossians 2:9 NKJV).

Many New Age members call Christ "the Master," but have already cleverly redefined Christian terms. They mean that He, as a mortal man, ascended in seven or less reincarnations to the state of a master, a guru. In so doing they have made it appear as if He had gained His elevated state by works, which denies His deity.

In addition the New Age movement denies Christ's atonement, because it does not teach that He suffered and died as a mediator on the cross, but that he swooned. Further, they teach He ascended from the grave by His own willpower, thereby making His own reality.

Concerning His death, Scripture tells us, "But God demonstrates His own love toward us, in that while we were still sinners, Christ died for us" (Romans 5:8 NKJV). Further Jesus Christ was ". . . declared to be the Son of God with power, according to the Spirit of holiness, by the resurrection from the dead" (Romans 1:4 NKJV). He was God, but He did not do his own resurrecting. ". . . Just as Christ was raised from the dead by the glory of the Father . . ." (Romans 6:4). The two other parts of the trinity became involved in it.

Christianity says good works result from God's grace, His favor. But like many religious movements, the New Age movement says salvation comes about through works. It purports that we ascend to a god state through our actions, and since it might take more than a lifetime to achieve this, reincarnation allows added opportunities to reach that goal.

Perhaps no passage of Scripture more descriptively relates to the New Age movement than Romans 1:21–23 (NKJV): ". . . although they knew God, they did not glorify Him as God, nor were thankful, but became futile in their thoughts, and their foolish hearts were darkened. Professing to be wise, they became fools, and changed the glory of the incorruptible God into an image made like corruptible man. . . ."

PART II
THE LION WITH MANY FACES

FOUR
THE LURE
OF SATAN

Leaving the west side of Chicago, Dr. Charles Scudder—a pharmacologist employed by a branch of the Loyola University school of medicine—and his homosexual partner of seventeen years, Joseph Odom, headed south for a tract of land in the southern Appalachian Mountains. Dr. Scudder had bought forty acres of mountaintop land completely surrounded by national forest. The companions planned to build their own copy of a thirteenth-century continental castle in which to live and worship Satan.

Six years later, I followed a rutted road toward their castle called Corpswood. Rounding the last bend, I came upon the manor, a large brick building designed to keep out intruders. Massive steel utility doors formed the castle's entrance. Two of the four chimneys bore satanic pentacles; a large, handmade stained-glass window over the courtyard showed a pentacle with a goat's head in the center.

Inside, the building looked like a satanic museum. The master bed, from the Italian Renaissance, held replicas of human skulls in indentations on its heavily carved headboard. Real skulls were stationed around the room.

The eerie sitting room held many volumes on satanism and witchcraft. In the dining room a picture showed a man with several head wounds, bound and gagged. When a friend asked Scudder about the work of art, he said, "That's how I'm going to die."

Later the friend reported, "He told me he saw how he was going to die in a vision. He said he had a demon following him around."

On my visit, I saw two large bloodstains, one in the kitchen and the other in the study. They marked the floor, where the castle's occupants had been shot to death by two young men who visited them often and traded sexual favors for homemade wine. The assailants had never seen the painting or heard of the demonic prophecies they had unwittingly fulfilled.

Scudder's body, bound and gagged, with gunshot wounds to the head, lay near the picture that depicted his fate. More than twenty spent shells littered the floor.

Those who doubt that satanism is an active force in America today need only look at the statistics. Groups called covens usually consist of nine to thirteen members, though they may have more. Authorities estimate there were approximately 10,000 covens in America in 1946, 48,000 by 1976, and 135,000 by 1985. The number grows daily.[1] Satanists grew from 480,000 in 1976, to 1.4 million in 1985, according to the February-March, 1987, issue of *National Sheriff*, a law enforcement publication.[2]

No one can claim immunity; satanism functions both in metropolitan areas and remote regions. A coven of twenty-two members functions in McComb, Mississippi. Local sheriff Robert Lawson said, "There are a number of sacrificial cults that exist. Some sacrifice animals, others humans."[3] In a television-journalism report aired in October, 1988, Geraldo Rivera interviewed people who had become part of satanic groups across America. He told the sad stories of many young people, on both coasts and in the Bible belt, who had become part of the movement.[4]

The Satan of the New Age

According to New Age proponents, Satan has been misunderstood and misrepresented. The movement teaches he was sent to earth, from Venus, 17 to 18.5 million years ago, as the supreme "ordering force." His assignment was to lead mankind on its evolutionary path back to god consciousness, that is, order. Supposedly the Cosmic Hierarchy assigned him the role of becoming a bridge between mankind and God.

New Age spokesman David Spangler defines the devil's role more specifically:

> Lucifer prepares man in all ways for the experience of Christhood and Christ prepares man for the experience of God. Jesus said, "As the Christ, I am the way, the truth and the life. No man goes to the Father but through me." This is true. The avenue out of microcosmic limitation into macrocosmic wholeness, universal consciousness and attunement is through the Christ. But the light that reveals to us the presence of the Christ, the light that reveals to us the path to the Christ comes from Lucifer.[5]

Note that he used the name *Lucifer*, not *Satan*. New Agers believe that in medieval times people "thought up" a mythical character they named Satan, in order to frighten unenlightened people into obedience. They discovered the force of Lucifer's neutral energies and misused them by misrepresenting Lucifer, who suffers "pain and sorrow and anguish" over mankind's condition. Now Lucifer tries to enter the darkness with mankind and precipitate misery and pain in a noble attempt to cause persons to turn from the dark side of the force.

Evil, according to the New Age thinking, is "that which is willed malevolently." Proponents of this concept explain away the devil and attribute evil to people's desires. Against the background of "you create your own reality," they explain that every bad or evil thing that happens to you is something you wanted to happen.

Though few would overtly encourage satanism, New Age adherents do nothing to discourage it. Their easy-going concept of him cultivates an environment in which a benevolent Satan is worthy of worship. By taking his evil less than seriously, they have fallen into one of his traps.

Satan in Modern America

Jeffrey Burton Russell, professor of history at the University of California at Santa Barbara and an authority on the idea of the devil in Western civilization, traces current satanism to a rise in interest in the occult that began in the 1960s as part of the New Age counterculture. "The rash of appallingly degenerate crime, including the violation of children and the mutilation of animals, can be tolerated only in a society determined to deny at any cost the radical existence of evil," he commented.[6]

Geraldo Rivera's report included the testimony of numerous children who had been abused as part of satanic rituals and it showed the bodies of animal sacrifices. Yet despite the overwhelming sameness of the children's reports and the physical evidence provided by animal carcasses, the American judicial system remains tentative in its willingness to ascribe such acts to satanism.[7]

Theologian Joseph Haroutunian appraised the need for acceptance of a demonic reality and response to it by saying:

> In our day after several centuries of eclipse, the devil has returned as the "demonic," expressive of the depth and mystery of evil in the world, as against the view which sees evil as either caused by physical forces or as willed malevolently by man. . . . So long as men try to think adequately about temptation, the devil will be acknowledged for what he is, the quasi-personal father of lies, allied with death and sin, and a power in the world which only the living God can and does overcome by the gospel and "the Spirit of truth."[8]

Have we thought adequately about this? Do we know what we're up against?

What Do Satanists Believe?

To deal fairly with satanism, we need to divide it into its identifiable subgroups. There are basically seven:

Conventional satanists   Conformists
Clandestine satanists   Nonconformists
Community satanists   Open and public
Covert satanists   Fringe groups

Charlatan satanists   Youth gangs
Closet satanists   Isolated individuals
Crazy satanists   Psychotics

Conventional satanists might be called orthodox believers. They are secretive, dedicated, and structured. Much like the drug subculture, most covens network with others. Complex hierarchies exist within groups, and often the satanic line dates back for generations in a family. Devotees closely follow rules and rituals. Although this group never goes public, it plants the seeds for and encourages all other more visible satanic groups. The core group avoids a name or label.

These satanists detest Christianity, and their ritual mocks it by perverting and debasing Christian doctrines and ceremonies.

Clandestine satanists gather their beliefs from a variety of sources. Their eclectic precepts do not always simply pervert Christianity, and their beliefs are a convergence of a number of magico-religious beliefs. They believe in a series of reincarnations on earth, to allow them to fully satisfy their carnal instincts.

Often cannabalistic, they believe that in eating the flesh or drinking the blood of a sacrifice, they receive from the victim an invisible force called manna. Some suppose they can gain immortality by eating the heart of a victim.

Community satanists are not underground. Society knows them best because they have public visibility. Although they do not give open endorsement to sacrifices, like conventional satanists, their rituals reverse and pervert Christianity. Some of the major community satanists in America include:

Church of All Worlds
Temple of Truth
Shrine of Sothis
Nemeton
Order of Thelema
Process Church of the Final Judgment
Order of the Circle
The Chingons
The Four P Movement
Brotherhood of the Ram
Ordo Templi Orientis (OTO)
The Satan Senate[9]

Covert satanists are fringe groups that use satanism as a focal point for a variety of deviant behaviors. Satanism has a more or less incidental role compared to their primary interests, such as pedophilia, sadomasochism, sex groups, or homosexuality. Their not very well defined beliefs regarding Satan vary from group to group.

Charlatan satanists are primarily youth gangs, which lack the sophistication of other elements in the satanic community. These "dabblers" tend to weave satanic overtones into their otherwise bizarre attitudes and actions. They borrow from various subculture conduct and are inclined to use satanism to justify their actions.

Despite their dabbler status, such groups are as dangerous to designated victims as orthodox satanists. However, they seem to attract more public attention than the secretive orthodox satanists.

Self-styled groups of charlatan satanists often consist of young people looking for the optimum form of rebellion against society. They may first indicate an interest in the occult through a preoccupation with satanic heavy-metal music, fantasy role-playing games, and an interest in drugs and deviant subculture peer groups. More aggressive members become defiant about their beliefs, wearing clothes and jewelry with blatant death, anarchy, satanic, and self-destructive themes.

Closet satanists practice the art alone. They might not know of local groups or perhaps feel shy about group involvement. They often tailor their beliefs to their own needs and desires.

Crazy satanists are psychotic persons who have been attracted to the bizarre aspect of satanism. Most are mentally deranged, though some are demon possessed. Often other groups exclude such individuals because they fear being exposed by or publically linked to them.

Eternity and the Satanist

Regarding their views on eternity, we can divide satanists into four schools of thought:

> *Reincarnation* is popular among many. Those adhering to this concept believe life is a series of

71

reincarnations intended to let them fulfill all their lustful desires. They look upon life as rather base, sensuous, and selfish.

Annihilation, the idea that when a person dies he or she ends existence in any state of being, motivates some. They believe there is no afterlife.

Vindication seems the most gratifying concept to some. These satanists believe Satan will eventually defeat the Christian God and gleefully rule throughout eternity. Thus they will emerge as victors in the spirit world.

Condemnation is readily conceded by many. They believe the Christian God will eventually defeat Satan in accordance with the Bible's teaching, and they will be condemned to hell. However, in this state of punishment, they expect to revel in their perpetual rebellion against God. Like spoiled children who become even more obstinate when disciplined, they conceive of themselves as further hardening their hearts. They forget that even the most rebellious child has a breaking point.

Marks of a Satanist

Entering the door leading to our church's office suite, I noted what appeared to be a simple Nazi swastika, along with some other markings, on the right door. When I called it to the attention of others, none thought that it signified anything more than the group in World War II Germany.

Hitler had adopted this sign from Hinduism, in which it stood for the four primary elements: fire, earth, water, and wind. However, it has now become a satanic mark.

Like everything else in satanism, it perverts something related to the Christian faith. As the ancient Jews placed blood on the doorposts of their homes as an indication to the angel of death to pass over them, the satanist places marks on a building he desires to curse. More than innocent scribbling, the marks had been placed there the day a small group of New Age, animal-rights loyalists had picketed our church.

Some symbols and signs used by occult adherents appear in Chart 1. Many of them I found throughout Corpswood.

Chart 1
Occult Symbols and Signs

The moon and star together represent the moon goddess, Diana, and the morning star, Lucifer. This is one of many symbols used by both white witchcraft and satanism. Satanists usually face the moon in the opposite direction.

With the circle this is known as a pentagram, and without the circle is called a pentacle. It is used in black and white magic.

An upside-down pentagram is known as a Baphomet or goat's head. It is used exclusively by satanists.

The seal of Solomon or hexagram is believed to be one of the most powerful symbols of the occult.

The "mark of the beast" or "sign of Satan" is represented four different ways. The letter *F* is the sixth in the alphabet.

The horned hand is innocently used by many people, but it is a sign of recognition among those involved in the occult.

The broken cross or swastika is of ancient origin, having been used by Hindus and the American Indians before being adopted by Hitler in World War II. It represents the four points of the compass, the four seasons, and the four winds. The turning of the ends indicates all have turned against mankind.

The symbol of anarchy depicts the abolition of all law. Heavy-metal enthusiasts use this symbol, which was first used by punk-rock groups.

The upside-down cross is intended to blaspheme the Christian cross. It is often worn in the ear or around the neck by rock musicians.

The cross of Nero was used in the early 1960s as a peace symbol. It is now used to symbolize the defeat of Christianity.

The upside-down ax is a perversion of an old Roman symbol, which originally stood for Roman justice. In Roman use the double-bladed ax was upright. Inverted, it now stands for antijustice.

In conjuring rituals the "triangle" is drawn where a demon is supposed to appear.

The circle has several meanings and usages. It symbolizes eternity. It is a protection from evil from without and of power within. In ritual use it is nine feet in diameter.

The amulet or talisman is used for inscribing the name or image of a supernatural power. The Lesser Key of Solomon lists most of these gods.

This diagram shows an altar, which is usually placed within a nine-foot circle. The central pentagram is usually carved. Human or animal blood is poured on the image.

Black Mass symbol.

Blood ritual symbol.

Occult words.

Nema   Natas   Redrum

Amen   Satan   Murder

Special Occult Holidays. Both satanists and witches celebrate eight major Sabbats annually. Satanists also hold a member's birthday as a special day. Activity usually increases around these days. The most significant ones are marked with an asterisk.

February 2	Ormelc or Candlemas
March 21	Equinoxes (1)
* April 30	Beltane or May Eve
* June 22	Solstice (1)
August 1	Lammas or August
September 21	Equinoxes (2)
* October 31	Halloween
* December 22	Solstice (2)

Who Are These People?

Unperturbed by the late hour and the slight chill in the spring air, a group of forty people gathered at a former Civil War site, under the full Georgia moon. One of them, Arlene, had always been a "religious" person, though not a Christian. Standing in the moonlight, she reflected that in less than thirty-six hours she would sit in church with her family. Arlene shivered in the cold air with the excitement of attending this "different" kind of worship service for the first time. She had come for a satanic service this night.

As she waited, various persons brought predesigned stones that they fitted together to form an altar. Satanic priests, attired in black-hooded robes, performed a preliminary ritual.

Then a young mother, clothed in the same kind of robe, approached the priests, carrying her baby. Pausing, she hesitatingly presented him to a priest. He and others used black leather straps to tie the infant to the altar of immolation. The tight thongs depressed the infant's tender flesh. Arlene's heart quickened and was compassionately moved at the sounds of his crying. *All he wants is for someone to hold and cuddle him*, Arlene thought instinctively.

Frenzied chants and prayers rose from the crowd as the high priest moved toward the altar, brandishing a sword. Arlene gasped and whispered to her satanic boyfriend, "They are not going to . . . to . . . , are they?"

With a fiendish chuckle, he replied, "You better believe they are!"

As the incantations reached a fever pitch, the priest stood before the altar and slowly raised his razor-sharp sword. In a swift second Arlene had witnessed the decapitation of her first satanic sacrifice.

According to Arlene, amid the tumult, a sudden flash of red and black smoke appeared in front of the altar. From it emerged the devil incarnate. Dogs quit barking, crickets were silenced, and for the moment all nature seemed transfixed. The crowd hushed.

The devil's well-formed, muscular body stood nearly seven feet tall; he had a grotesque face. Turning from the human sacrifice, he glared at the crowd, and the very ground seemed to quake. After giving an approving, guttural grunt, signifying his acceptance of the sacrifice, he moved toward the altar and was out of sight in an instant, amid the ardent appeals to Satan voiced by the crowd.

Did Arlene really see the devil? According to the author of one occult manual: "The spirit or force which is summoned in the ceremony is normally invisible. It can appear visibly to the magician (occultist, yogi, witch, satanist) by fastening on a source of energy on the physical plane of existence. It may do this by taking possession of one of the human beings involved in the ritual."[10]

Arlene is certainly convinced she saw a spirit manifestation of the devil.

Why do satanists offer human sacrifices? The same

manual provides this explanation: "In the latter grimoires the sacrifice is done . . . to increase the supply of force in the circle. In occult theory a living creature is a storehouse of energy, and when killed most of this energy is suddenly liberated. . . . The amount of energy let loose when the victim is killed is very great, out of all proportion to the animal's (or victim's) size or strength."[11] The energy it talks about, also called shakti, is intensified by mind shocks such as ritual orgies, which occur at the same time as the sacrifice.

Why would that young mother offer her child as a sacrifice? Because she sought favors from Satan, Arlene explained. Within days, the mother had the new car she desired. Other young friends from the coven gleefully spoke of becoming pregnant and sacrificing their babies. Arlene and many other strikingly attractive young girls frequently participated in satanic orgies, hoping to conceive a child for Satan. The coven held such orgies indoors or outside, and no one felt any shyness about participating in open group sex with anyone, at any time, in any way.

During the following months, Arlene became increasingly involved in satanism. She learned to speak backwards, to recite certain rituals. Her group had taught Arlene that when she first met a person she should immediately think of how to kill him or her, if necessary. The coven also taught her how to cast spells, sometimes using the bones from sacrifices. They even taught her how to dress seductively.

Although she attended the satanic services, the

"communion services" and sacrifices left Arlene nauseated. The entire "communion service" debased the Lord's Supper by replacing the fruit of the vine with a sacrificial victim's blood and soaking the wafer in its urine.

Arlene's next worship included the sacrifice of a twelve-year-old girl, who knew what was about to happen and pathetically cried to God for help. The group enjoyed her pleas, since they believed it evidenced the superiority of their god. The high priest achieved the child's death with a swift blow to the heart.

Observing how skillfully they dissected and dismembered bodies, Arlene concluded some of the priests must have had medical training. Later she learned she was correct; indeed, some of them were in health-care professions.

Arlene's third sacrifice explained her reluctance to break with the group. A lovely young woman of about twenty-five had been turned in by her "friends" as a would-be defector. Ceremonially the priests tied her to the altar, and the same priest pierced her heart with a sword. Swiftly he began to skin the victim. While life still quivered in the flesh, he bit into and chewed it as he turned to face an approving crowd. It was as if he had said to Arlene, *If you try to leave our group, this will be your fate also.*

Was this an isolated, radical incident? I told Arlene that Larry Dunn, a Washington State sheriff's deputy and member of the Cult Crime Impact Network, estimates as many as 50,000 human sacrifices take place every year in America.[12] "Do you think there are that many?" I asked. "More," she told me and went on to relate that each group has to have thirty-three sacrifices (one for each year of Christ's earthly life) on the Friday and Saturday before Easter. Many may be animals, but at least one must be a human sacrifice. On other occasions a similar number of sacrifices are required. In our own unsuspecting community, she told me, four groups met one night to offer human sacrifices.

How did they dispose of the remains of sacrifices? Some were eaten, or participants took flesh and blood home for later use. Bodies were also burned and the remains thrown in a river or lake. She showed me aerial photographs of abandoned rural churches where covens performed their rites. Each church had a cemetery, where the groups could open old graves and bury the remains of sacrifices.

"Arlene, I have one final question. What would you say to any person considering getting involved in satanism?"

Without hesitating, she answered, "Don't!" Then she told me of lingering emotional stress and fear for her life, her legacy from leaving the group. Only after forty-five hours of prayer by friends was she freed from demonic manifestations. Knowing the danger to her life, she thrust herself upon the Lord, asking His protective custody in her life. God has been faithful, but one of Arlene's friends who tried another route out is missing and presumed caught and sacrificed.

Authorities indicate that the public would be amazed at the cross-segment of society involved in satanism. Wayne VanKampen, chief pastoral officer at Denver's Bethesda Hospital, identifies the typical satanic worshiper as an underachiever, suffering from low self-esteem, experiencing conflict with peers and alienation from family and its religion. Such a person is likely to be intelligent, creative, white, and upper middle class. Because masochism is part of satanism, young girls often do not find it appealing; instead they may turn to witchcraft.[13]

Indications of an inordinate interest in or involvement with satanism include an obsession with heavy-metal music, fantasy role-playing, extensive reading on the occult, unexplained paranoia, drug use, keeping an occult journal, or using an inverted pentagram or other satanic symbols.[14]

Many parents are not close enough to their children to observe these tell-tale signs, but those who relate warmly with their children may become aware of some. In response they should not simply take away the objects that reveal involvement in the occult. Instead they should discuss the problem, using loving logic to help their children see the wisdom of not following this line of thought and practice.

Children of Fear

But not all members of satanic groups are rebellious young people. Some are trapped in homes where the

religion is practiced. Out of fear and because of intimi-
dation they remain mute and often become scarred.
Meet one, whose name is Rodney.

The night I baptized him, I asked Rodney if he had
any family. In an emotional response made in an effort
to keep that moment special, he answered, "Not that I
know of." Within days, though, he called and asked me
for counsel.

Gradually Rodney opened his painful past and
shared that he was actually part of a large family that
was involved in satanism. In the basement of their
suburban house his father had kept a small room
filled with cats and dogs destined for use in satanic
worship.

Because they knew something strange went on
around Rodney's house, other children stayed away, so
the animals in "the pit" became his closest companions.
Knowing their fate made him feel sorry for them.

When he was eight, Rodney was unwillingly drawn
into the coven over which his dad presided. At midnight
they met in the basement or in a wooded area. Animals
were skinned alive and their blood drained for use as a
base for drugs. Ritualistically, they drank it.

Rodney remained silent about the coven. He had
witnessed his father beat his mother with a hammer and
threaten her in an effort to keep her silent. In separate
ceremonies he had seen two of his brothers have their
heads cut off with an ax. Later, when their bodies were
found, his father claimed they had been victims of
murder.

As a special day of satanic celebration approached, Rodney became aware that he would be the next sacrifice. He broke the chains of fear and family loyalty and fled for his life. His father was arrested and later convicted of murder.

Briefly Rodney felt hope when the state placed him in a foster home, but terror struck when he discovered his foster parents were also satanists. Again he ran away and became a street child. Compassionate Christians found him in a public shelter, starved for love. They built a bridge of trust to Rodney, and he accepted Christ. Today joy characterizes Rodney's life. He needs to run no more, because his best friend is the Lamb.

However, not all stories end as happily as Rodney's. Mary called my office to receive help with problems with her children. Reluctantly she consented to come to the church. Seated outside on a picnic bench, she told her whole story without making eye contact with me. Guilt and fear had haunted her since, at age six, she had been abused by her father. Initially against her will, she began to participate in satanic rituals. At first repelled by the things the coven participated in, she began to enjoy them. Eventually she became pregnant by someone, though she did not know whom. At her optimum moment of commitment, she sacrificed her child as part of an invocation for a certain demon to enter her.

Years later the sacrifice still haunted her. But the

entrenchment in satanism had such a lasting grip on Mary's life that we could never guide her to an acceptance of Christ. She never found the peace she hoped to gain.

Kathy Snowden, a psychotherapist from Richmond, Virginia, estimates that 250 therapists nationwide work with satanist ritual abuse cases. One clinical psychologist alone reports treating as many as thirty victims on a regular basis.[15]

Most satanists believe man is inherently selfish, violent, and sensual. They think they should express or even celebrate the natural attributes of hate, lust, and greed. Because they do not believe in sin and guilt, their consciences do not trouble them. What Christians call the seven deadly sins they consider commendable; they are encouraged to practice at least one a day to aid relaxation.

Satanists do not have a passive attitude toward Christians. They consider them weak and soft, because of their charity, benevolence, and forgiveness. Society, they say, is made weak by Christians, because they refuse to get rid of those who should be disposed of. Satanism uses many of these "disposable" people as ritual sacrifices.

Crime and Satanism

Knowing that satanists have such an outlook, we should not feel surprise at their connection with crime.

Arlene told me her coven used criminal activities to keep control over members who might otherwise have left. By the time they wanted out, the leaders had so much against them that the members dared not take a step away.

Some days it seems impossible to pick up a newspaper that doesn't have a report on occult-related crime. Often the perpetrators seem to be teens who perform murder to seek the favor of the devil. But we may never know how much crime has a relationship to satanism.

Estimates on its extent vary. For instance, Sandi Gallant, a police spokeswoman on the subject, finds the estimate of 50,000 human sacrifices a year grossly exaggerated, yet she admits authorities have no way to accurately judge statistics.[16] Even those who doubt the figures often do not doubt that satanism *has* had a powerful impact on America's increase in crime.

Not every law-enforcement agency agrees on this issue. Divided on the issue, the FBI does not officially acknowledge cult-related crime.[17] However, many police officers—some within the FBI—speak out loudly concerning its reality. According to one expert, many police personnel already involved in dealing with occult crime are Christians.[18]

While avoiding the scare tactics some have used or advocated, Christians must realize that a relationship between crime and satanism does exist and treat it accordingly. Whether or not the FBI makes a decision in the near future, Christians know the guns and personnel they provide may still prove largely useless. This is a spiritual battle, one won only in Christ. As the legal officials battle on their front, we must man the prayer lines.

FIVE

SATAN'S MEDIA

Satanism has employed all conceivable means to reach the minds of men. Movies, novels, television, and the lecture circuit all have been utilized to voice the satanic "gospel."

Often satanists hang around theaters showing late-night occult movies. They know the persons who attend have a basic interest in the occult, and they simply wait for them to reveal it. Satanists cultivate friendships or even approach strangers, inviting them to a party after the movie. There they introduce people to some superficial satanic acts and principles. If they show further interest, they are gradually introduced to hard-core satanism.

Satanists may make similar pickups around record shops that display black (occult) heavy-metal music. As a youth browses through them, the "evangelizers" know they have a prospect.

Select in their proselytizing, satanists wait for a candidate to show interest. Patiently they prepare him before introducing him to a coven. By the time he is ready for induction, they have involved him in so many incriminating acts, he can't back out for fear of exposure.

Satanic Music

According to Carl Raschke, director of Denver Institute of Humanities, heavy-metal music is to the self-styled satanist what gospel music is to Christianity. Heavy-metal music is a powerful reinforcement that legitimizes the occult.[1]

It's hard to tell if the music industry exploits satanism or satanism exploits the music industry. Either way, through music, the themes of satanism—self-mutilation, assault, mayhem, suicide, drugs, murder, sex, and rebellion—have gone public. Freedom, irresponsibility, and violence recur in the message of this music.

Most persons agree that such music is not the basic cause, but a stimulus and occasion for satanic involvement. Many youth, involved in personal or emotional problems, have had the music become "the straw that broke the camel's back."

Donald Sparry, director of Brunswick's Coastal Georgia Police Academy and an authority on violent extremism said, "A lot of kids are buying into violence. Take a violent attitude, following a violent philosophy, combining that with alcohol and drugs [and putting it] in the hands of adolescents who are already unstable . . . [causes] you [to] have a formula for disaster."[2] Considering the violent message of satanic heavy-metal music, it's not hard to imagine it can become part of such a disaster.

Heavy metal consists of power chords, screaming electric guitars, throat-wrenching screams and shouts, and overly dramatic drumming. It has three basic classes:

> *Party/Glam metal* is sex, drug, and party oriented.
> *Thrash metal* encourages hatred and negative attitudes toward authority.
> *Black metal* is occult and satanic in nature. It is identified by leather, chains, sadomasochism, and domination over females.

Punk rock is raw, abrasive, basic, and fast. Within this style is occult punk, which involves witchcraft, spells, and satanic ritual. Much of the music focuses on death, gloom, and suicide.[3]

If as a parent you observe your child absorbed in such music, take action. This does not mean simply removing records or tapes, nor does it mean merely asking your child to turn down the volume. Instead, go in and listen to the words, without requesting a volume adjustment. Confront your child with calm, controlled conversation about the content of the music, instead of making frontal assaults that tend to close conversation. Later pick a time when your child is in a proper mood and ask questions that will enable him or her to see the negative aspects of such music. Read about the groups your child listens to, so that you can ask questions that will provide insight into the musicians' character.

Give posters of individuals or groups the same attention. These, too, are interest entry points into the occult.

Such action will require a large amount of patience on the part of parents, but it will encourage a child to give up such music, while keeping open the lines of communication. Time so invested will be well spent. Don't ignore the symptoms. Work at your overall relationship and provide time for positive experiences between you and your child. Interchange will produce more if the overall relationship is positive and loving.

Satanic Handbooks

On the last night of April, 1966—Walpurgisnacht, witchcraft's most important festival—Anton Szandor LaVey donned a clerical collar and presided over the first blasphemous assembly of the Satanic Church.[4] Today he bears the title the Black Pope of the Church of Satan.

Describing the works of others as a "sanctimonious fraud,"[5] LaVey set about writing his own manual on satanism, called *The Satanic Bible*. In it he systematized the philosophies of satanism, using such sources as:

Voodoo cults
Nineteenth-century England's Hell-Fire Club
Aleister Crowley's nineteenth-century satanic circle
The 1920s Black Order of Germany
The Knights Templar of fourteenth-century France
The Golden Dawn of nineteenth-century England

Although it offers nothing new, *The Satanic Bible* has rekindled the fire beneath an old broth. In it LaVey expounds satanism's philosophy more clearly and fully than any of his predecessors.

The Nine Satanic Statements that summarize the book advocate indulgence, vengeance, and personal gratification, in addition to identifying man as "just another animal" and demanding that people deserve kindness and always be responsible. Not only does it show a twisted duality that requires that one "deserve" grace, while advocating all that is opposite to it, it places man at the center of his universe, by continually forcing him to seek personal gratification of his lusts.

The book is divided into four major headings:

Fire	The Book of Satan
Air	The Book of Lucifer
Earth	The Book of Belial
Water	The Book of Leviathan

The physical elements stand for the original four elements of which men thought everything was made. Their use indicates the material, worldly nature of the volume. The names are classified by LaVey as "the Four Crown Princes of Hell."[6]

The first book, the only one written in chapter and verse form, at once parodies and perverts portions of the King James Version of the Bible. In addition it provides a decalogue on man's origin and object in life, from a satanic viewpoint.

The Book of Lucifer, a philosophical treatise on love, hate, satanic sex, indulgence, and human sacrifice, also provides some observations on this present day as the Age of Satan. Its observation that truth alone will never set men free and only doubt brings mental emancipation epitomizes the book.[7]

As a how-to section, LaVey provides the Book of Belial. Here he reveals theory and practice of satanic magic, types of satanic ritual, and the ingredients used in satanic magic. You might call it a satanic *McGuffey's Reader*.

The Book of Leviathan, "The Raging Sea," takes up the bulk of the volume. It is written in the alleged language of the satanic ritual, "Enochian." Although some claim this language is older than Sanskrit, it first appeared in written form in 1659. These Enochian Calls are satanic paeans of faith.

The Satanic Ritual

Since the release of *The Satanic Bible* resulted in a flood of related works, none of which LaVey felt met the needs of devotees, he followed its publication with *The Satanic Ritual*. As a second reason for writing it, LaVey cited new "discoveries" that afforded the sorcerer new tools with which to work. Finally, he said "magic . . . produces what one puts in it."[8] *The Satanic Ritual* is the "how, where, and when" of satanism. Graphically recording satanic methodology, it basically perverts and parodies much Roman Catholic ceremony. It substitutes obvious sensual, lustful, base, and secular elements to form the Black Mass.

"There is a demon inside man," LaVey is reported to have said. "It must be exercised, not exorcised— channeled into ritualized hatred."[9] *The Satanic Bible* and *The Satanic Ritual* are compilations of classic ways of exercising that demon.

SIX

BREAKING THE SPELL OF WITCHCRAFT

"I conjure Thee, O Circle of Power. . . ." As the slender priestess solemnly spoke these bewitching words, the twelve members of her coven stood reverently silent around the table altar in the center of the room. Brandishing the athame (ritual knife), she moved around the room, marking an imaginary circle on the floor as she continued to chant: ". . . that thou become a boundary between the world of men and the realms of the Mighty Ones."

Her green-robed companions remained absorbed in

her invocation of the Great Mother, Diana. Almost immediately the heretofore silent priest invoked the horned god Pan. Throughout the remainder of the ceremony the members of the coven, now inside the circle, looked upon these two officiants as representative embodiments of these deities.

The *World Christian Encyclopedia* estimates 6 million Americans profess to be witches and engage in practices like these. They are a subgroup of over 10 million persons the encyclopedia says call themselves pagans, who practice "primitive" religions such as Druidism, Odinworship, and Native American shamanism.[1]

According to Sergeant Lorie A. Johnson, founder of the Farwander Military Pagan Fellowship, these neopagans encompass such groups as the Wiccans, the Druids, the goddess worshipers, people who worship the Nordic-Celtic pantheons, the ancient Egyptian pantheons, and various native American beliefs. They parallel New Age philosophy in their belief in multiple deities as well as the oneness of all nature.[2]

What Is a Witch?

Our image of witches comes to us from the three hags in *Macbeth*, who stir their awful caldrons and mutter weird chants; from *Grimm's Fairy Tales*, where their long, crooked, warty fingers point at us while the witches cackle; from Sid and Marty Krofft, who filled our eyes with such monstrous females in their cartoons;[3] and from Witchiepoo chasing H. R. Pufenstuff around.

The reality is quite different. Not uncommonly, high school students can point to attractive young girls rumored to be witches. You might never have guessed it from the girls' appearance. They may live with their parents, go to church, and associate with adults from whom they hide their sorcery. Others have mainstream careers and go unnoticed by friends; they reveal their occult inclinations only to a close, appreciative inner circle.

According to witchcraft tradition, the goddess of the new year takes on the form of a maiden. As the year progresses, she takes on the form of a mother. In the fall, when things begin to wither and die, she takes on the appearance of an old crone. Most people think of this image when they think of a witch.[4] In reality, today's average witch is young, well educated, interested in science fiction, given to alternative lifestyles, and often has many pets. Leadership cadres tend to be in their late twenties and early thirties; members are usually in their early twenties. Approximately 50 percent come from Protestant backgrounds, 25 percent from Catholic backgrounds, and 10 percent from Jewish backgrounds. While growing up, few were active in their faith.[5]

Concerning her book *Diary of a Witch*, Sybil Leek commented on America's unexpected response to it: "I thought it would answer all the questioning on a subject which to me was very ordinary, for the simple reason that I had never known any other way of life or any other faith. What I really achieved was a kicking open of the door for many millions [yes, millions!] of people who wanted to know more about witchcraft, more and more."[6] The continued popularity of such books indicates that our country still has an interest in witchcraft.

What Do Witches Believe?

Witchcraft has a sort of brew-your-own "theology," because beliefs and practices greatly vary.

Like most of the New Age movement, witchcraft is pantheistic. Gordon Melton, director of the Institute for Study of American Religion at the University of California at Santa Barbara, said of witchcraft, "There is some polytheism there and it is all overlaid with Jungian philosophy, but the bottom line is that they worship nature. Christians consider nature to be dead, to be usable. Witches consider it to be alive, to be revered."[7]

Two practitioners of witchcraft, Bonnie and Lee Darrow, reflected New Age beliefs when they wrote, "We attempt to attune ourselves to the cosmic forces so that they may flow through us, and be directed to benefit ourselves and others in need of help."[8]

In addition:

> Most witches believe in a form of reincarnation that allows them several lives on earth to achieve purity. When they finally reach this pure state, they are re-

warded with everlasting unification with the "Ultimate Deity."[9]

They try to put themselves in harmony with nature through ritual. Many of their deities are hunting and fertility gods or goddesses. They believe the "creator god" cannot be known.

They cast spells, primarily by use of candles. Their handbooks describe spells and rituals, relating to such things as breaking up a love affair, overcoming a bad habit, putting pressure on others, healing an unhappy marriage, healing the sick, arousing jealousy, and winning love.

They believe one is born in innocence and becomes corrupted. They teach practitioners to earn their salvation by self-denial and fetish acts that enable them to be reincarnated into more perfect specimens.

They advocate many roads to their deities, through chanting, drugs, and meditation.

Roots of the Worship

Witches observe four holidays, one for each season:

Candlemas or Brigid's Day	February 2
May Eve	April 30
Lammas Eve	July 31
Halloween or All Hallows Eve	October 31

The earliest Halloween celebrations were held in honor of Samhain, lord of the dead, by the Druids, priests of ancient Gaul and Britain.[10] They believed cats were former human beings consigned to animal form as punishment for evil deeds. In addition their faith held that on Halloween, ghosts, spirits, witches, elves, and fairies came out to harm the living. From this come the basic symbols of Halloween.[11]

But the belief in the harm caused by such spirits was not limited to Gaul and Britain:

> There was a prevailing belief among all nations that at death the souls of good men were taken possession of by good spirits and carried to paradise, but the souls of wicked men were left to wander in the space between the earth and moon, or consigned to the unseen world. These wandering spirits were in the habit of haunting the living . . . but there were means by which these ghosts might be exorcised."[12]

To prevent spirits from doing their evil tricks, people commonly left out food and offered them shelter for the night.

Modern Worship

On Halloween, in a home in Long Island, a coven gathers to celebrate. They remove their clothes and bathe in salt water to purify themselves. Then, still sky clad, as they call it, they descend to the basement of the house and step inside a nine-foot circle, drawn about them with a four-hundred-year-old sword, by Mrs. Buckland, the high priestess, who is known in the craft as Lady Rowen. Music from a tape recorder and burning incense provide a bewitching ambience.

Within the circle, the witches sing, chant, dance with broomsticks in commemoration of an ancient fertility rite, drink tea and wine, and listen to the high priestess read from the *Book of Shadows*.

The ceremony ends after Lady Rowen, dressed in only a silver crown, bracelet, necklace, and green leather garter belt, places a horned helmet on the head of her husband, the high priest, known as Robat. Her action signifies that she has transferred her power, which she held for the six months of summer, to the high priest. He will rule throughout the winter.[13]

Modern sabbats closely resemble the ancient ritual, which entailed:

1. An oath of total commitment—body and soul—to the devil's service.
2. A promise to bring new members to the faith.
3. Eternal fealty and loyalty.
4. Sorcery and revenge against all opponents of the society.
5. A promise to sacrifice children under three years of age. [Generally modern witches deny such sacrifices, but many former witches testify they have seen them.]
6. A promise to split marriages.
7. Adoration of the devil by symbolically kissing his rump.
8. Receiving a box of ointments and magic powders.
9. A feast followed by dancing.
10. A sexual orgy that sometimes included incest.
11. Further eating and drunkenness.

    12. Beating those who had been remiss in their malevolent duties.

    13. Mass mockery of the sacraments of the church.[14]

Initiation ceremonies involve purification oaths, ordeals, and ultimately instruction in the creed. Modern witch candidates must swear an oath to secrecy. At the end, they are given new names to symbolize rebirth.[15]

Of the commitment required to become a witch, Sybil Leek stated: "I did not just wake up one morning and discover I was a witch. Witchcraft, like any other religion, must be accepted consciously. It is a decision that requires maturity."[16]

As evolution of interest occurs, occult ability, in the form of divination, psychic perception, healing ability, casting of spells or charming, increases. This requires belief, commitment, faith, dedication, and love, just as does the Christian faith.

Witchcraft *does* have power. Reading about some of the spells and charms may make them appear simple and trivial, unless we realize that demonic powers lie behind all forms of idolatry (1 Corinthians 10:20), including witchcraft. It takes faith in the art of Satan to receive his power and become his slave.

Whitewashing the Devil

Not all witches want to appear in this light. Protesting the connection of satanism with witchcraft, Selena Fox, a high priestess of the Church of the Circle of Wicca in Madison, Wisconsin, said, "Satanism is the opposite of witchcraft. We don't believe in evil practices, we abide by a love ethic. Harming any of Nature's creations is the last thing we'd ever do."[17]

One of the best-organized national orders of witchcraft, the Covenant of the Goddess (COG), has had legal recognition as a church since 1975. Part of its mission is to work with witches in public-image improvement. Its preamble says: "We are agreed: that we worship the Goddess and recognize the Old Gods; that we are ethical persons, bound by the ethics of the traditional Laws of our religion; and that we recognize each other as being members of the same religion." But their profession and practice clash. Their traditional laws allow them to cast spells evoking jealousy, breaking up families, and harming enemies. This religion is not as docile as they would have us believe.

Some witches claim they simply utilize powers unknown to man and do not identify the sources of that power. Others profess they have this power; it is satanic; and they do all by the power of Satan. Anton LaVey has no good words for those who would use his tools but not give Satan his due.[18] At least one can commend Mr. LaVey for his honesty on the subject!

Illusion or Witchcraft?

About 85 percent of what people bill as witchcraft is not that at all. It is a farce that uses illusion—floating tables, levitating heads, suspended girls, mysteriously vanishing and reappearing objects and individuals. All

NEW AGE, THE OCCULT, AND LION COUNTRY

these can be artistically accomplished without use of occult powers. Some "witchcraft" may also result from psychological factors.

But what of the 15 percent that does not come from such sources? I have seen levitation that could not have used illusionists' devices. In addition, some psychics actually move things from one place to another. In Tibet, in their acts of worship, some people have been reported reciting long passages of Shakespeare, knowing nothing of the author and never having heard his language![19]

The Bible says this 15 percent *does* exist and gives us a clear picture of the reality of witchcraft. It has spoken often on the subject, but it also shows that witchcraft does not overpower God (*see* Chart 2 for a few examples).

Remember, that Jesus took Satan on one-on-one when the devil tempted Him in the wilderness of Judea. What a clash that must have been, for Jesus encountered a one-time friend in Lucifer, "the light bearer," who had been a radiant angel in heaven, before his fall. By the power of heaven, Christ emerged the victor from the blandishments of the tempter.

During Christ's earthly ministry, demonic influence manifested itself more greatly than at any other time in history. As His Second Coming draws nearer, Satan becomes all the more restless, rebellious, and ruthless; and the demonic hordes become more expressive and aggressive.

Demons have far greater capacities than humans, and

Chart 2
Biblical Accounts of Witchcraft

Bible Reference	Act	Result
1 Kings 18	Queen Jezebel practiced witchcraft.	Israel had no peace as long as she lived and practiced witchcraft.
2 Kings 21; 2 Chronicles 33	Manasseh practiced witchcraft.	Judah was conquered by Assyria until he repented.
Acts 8:13	Simon the Sorceror confronted Paul and performed magical feats.	Simon understood that Paul's power was greater than his and sought it.
Acts 13:8–11	Elymas the Sorceror sought to turn Sergius Paulus from Paul's testimony.	Through Paul, he was struck blind by the Holy Ghost.
Acts 19:17–20	New Christians confessed their witchcraft and burned their occult books.	"Mightily grew the word of God and prevailed" (v. 20).

anyone who tries to take them on singlehandedly makes a grave mistake. However, they are far inferior to the powers of heaven. Through faith in the Lord Jesus Christ, no Christian has any cause to fear demonic forces. Scripture states, "For God hath not given us the spirit of fear; but of power, and of love, and of a sound mind" (2 Timothy 1:7). The fear we experience is not from Him.

SEVEN

ANGELS OF DARKNESS OR LIGHT?

About a year after he had decided the devil was not real, William D. Eisenhower had a spiritual encounter with a demon. It was "too real to deny, but too incongruous with my view of the world to accept." He described the encounter:

I was alone and suddenly felt that someone was staring at me. I turned to look. There was no one there—that I could see—and yet I knew that 12 feet away, at a very definite spot, a dark entity was glaring at me. Somehow

I could tell that it hated me with a wild, pent-up, frustrated intensity. Trusting my eyes, I turned back around and thought, "How odd. There's no one there." Yet the awareness of the dark presence did not go away, and I became terrified. A few seconds later, I ran from the scene in panic.[1]

Even after that experience, Eisenhower did not accept a personal devil, though he believed in a personal God. It took time and many other factors to bring him to a realization that his view of Satan had been too restricted. Today he believes in a very real, active devil.

Who Are These Angels?

Scripture does not specifically detail the creation of Satan, but most scholars accept two passages, Ezekiel 28:11–17 and Isaiah 14:12–15, which describe the kings of Tyre and Babylon, as referring to Satan's fall. Such dualistic reference is not uncommon in the Bible.

Ezekiel's passage refers to the king of Tyre but also seems to describe a being with abilities beyond that of man. The king seems to be referred to only in a graphic, figurative sense. If we apply this passage to Satan, it describes him as "full of wisdom, and perfect in beauty" (v. 12). Yet this perfectly created being became the originator of sin: "Thou wast perfect in thy ways from the day that thou wast created, till iniquity was found in thee" (v. 15).

Isaiah describes the fall of Lucifer. In five "I will"

passages, the prophet relates the rebellion of the angel of light who became Satan, "the adversary."

When an English Bible uses the word *devil*, it translates the Greek word *diabolos*, which refers to Satan. *Devils*, plural, translates the word *daimon*, signifying a demon of lesser authority. Such angels fell with Satan, because they had sided with him, against God.

What Can They Do?

Theologian Charles Hodge warns:

As to the power and agency of these evil spirits, they are represented as being exceedingly numerous, as everywhere efficient, as having access to our world, and as operating in nature and in the minds of men. We must take the Scriptures in their plain historical sense, or we do thereby reject them as a rule of faith. Evil spirits do exist. They have access to the minds and bodies of men. Why should we refuse to believe on the authority of Christ that they were allowed to have special power over men? The world, since the Apostasy, belongs to the kingdom of Satan; and to redeem it from his dominion was the special object of the mission of the Son of God. We are not to deny what is plainly recorded in the Scriptures as facts on this subject; we have no right to assert that Satan and his angels do not now in any case produce similar effects.[2]

Satan and his demons are active in many ways. They seek to:

> Control the lives of unbelievers (Ephesians 2:2–4) and draw them into the occult.
> Tempt Christians to sin.

Because they are created beings and do not have unlimited sway over the earth, Satan and the demons cannot go beyond certain powers, but they may:

> Afflict people with bodily diseases (Luke 13:16). This does not imply that *all* diseases are demonic in origin, but some result from demon influence in a person's life.
> Dispense error among people and seek to reduce believers' effectiveness (2 Peter 2:1).
> Seek to convince people they can talk with the dead (1 Samuel 28:7–25).
> Tempt people with unclean thoughts (Mark 5:13).
> Be stronger than human beings (Luke 8:29).

Since He created them, Satan and his minions cannot overcome Christ. Because He has authority over all things, Jesus can defeat them each time, as He did when He came to earth: "And having spoiled principalities and powers [this refers to demonic forces], he made a shew of them openly, triumphing over them in it" (Colossians 2:15). That triumph was the resurrection.

During His earthly ministry, the Bible repeatedly tells

112

us of Christ's casting out demons. Was He simply going along with the superstitions of the day? Did He merely call a physical illness or an emotional disturbance a demon? Or did Jesus know the power of Satan and deal with it directly? To answer that, I'd like to share my own experience and a professional opinion.

As our worship service drew to an end, I looked up to see a mammoth man walking down the aisle. I had heard of such a person disturbing church services in Atlanta and gave a signal to two of our men. Calmly they came to stand nearby as the "guest" asked me for the privilege of giving a brief word of testimony. In keeping with his pattern in other churches, he began by praising the Lord, but soon it deteriorated into profanity, vulgarity, and speaking a nonlanguage.

By this time my aides had grasped his arms and were tugging unsuccessfully at them. The guest's eyes had become transfixed, and froth dribbled from the corners of his mouth.

Stepping directly in front of him, until his face was less than six inches from mine, I prayed aloud, "Dear Jesus, I ask You by the power of Your Blood shed on Calvary, in the authority You have over all forces of evil, to command this voice to cease, to shut up. I ask You to control the demons at work here now."

Instantly the giant went mute. My aides, each weighing over 250 pounds, later told me that until that moment they had been unable to budge him. As the man became silent he also went limp, and they gently led him away.

Some weeks later, when I was in a group of people the incident came up in conversation. One, a doctor, had some familiarity with the case and explained that the man's actions had no medical or mental reasons. "I don't profess to know anything about demons," he warned us. "But if I have ever seen a case of possession, that has to be it."

Satan's Recruits

It all starts with some interest in the occult. When Satan finds someone open to it, he lures him along as if he had a fish on his line. By cultivating the interest and offering baits to attract him, Satan draws him near.

One spiritist reported that initially she saw a soft glow in her room at night. Each time her husband awakened, the glow vanished. Soon a face replaced it, but again, it disappeared when her husband awoke. Her husband encouraged the woman to speak to the image when it next appeared. The progression continued, and she now possesses a variety of psychic abilities.[3]

Mitch joined the navy to see the world, but he didn't get a very good view from a submarine. Difficulty with social relationships, disillusionment with Christianity, and indulgence in alcohol, combined with loneliness, drove him to seek group activities. That's how he became involved in Dungeons & Dragons, a fantasy game that opens the door to the occult.

He advanced through all seven manuals, becoming a proficient dungeon master. In his free time, Mitch developed his Dungeons & Dragons character, until its traits began to show in his own personality. After a friend became hospitalized because of emotional problems resulting from overidentification with the game, Mitch assessed its dangers, renounced it, and embraced Christianity. He concluded the role playing the game required was its greatest danger. Through it he had been brought closer and closer to the occult.

Although some have praised the game for its ability to encourage creative thinking, Pat Pulling, director of Bothered About Dungeons & Dragons, doesn't agree. Her son's death was incited by the game. "Let me destroy any myths," she says. "Most people don't commit suicide or murder when they play this game. But there are living kids having significant emotional problems because they can't get out of the role playing.

"All players must pledge allegiance to one or more deities, many of which come from the occult world. They are taught how to conjure demons and how to perform human sacrifice."[4] In the game, players pledge allegiance to Egyptian and Indian gods. This should turn any worshiper of the True and Living God against the game.[5]

Withdrawal from playing Dungeons & Dragons, especially if forced, should be accompanied by love and reassurance. The person discontinuing the game should be watched, to be certain no adverse emotional reactions result.

Combating Demonic Forces

Don't Become Involved

If you are not involved with the occult, avoid it! Scripture gives us a clear warning.

> Wherefore, my dearly beloved, flee from idolatry. . . . What say I then? that the idol is any thing, or that which is offered in sacrifice to idols is any thing? But I say, that the things which the Gentiles sacrifice, they sacrifice to devils. . . .
>
> 1 Corinthians 10:14, 19, 20

When William Eisenhower fled from the confrontation with a demon, he was not far wrong. Getting involved with such things is dangerous work, unless one confronts the devil in the power of Christ!

If You Are Involved, Turn From It

When Mitch turned from Dungeons & Dragons, he followed the advice of God's Word by "casting down imaginations, and every high thing that exalteth itself against the knowledge of God, and bringing into captivity every thought to the obedience of Christ" (2 Corinthians 10:5). Those who know Christ need not become involved in any occult activity. Knowing that

116

Jesus shed His blood for them, they can rely upon Him for guidance and to control their lives. He has "delivered them from the power of darkness" (*see* Colossians 1:13).

James promises that if we submit ourselves to God, the devil will flee from us (4:7). Until we submit to His lordship, we confront the devil alone and will lose every time. When we submit to Christ, He confronts the devil, who can do nothing but flee. Christ is triumphant!

EIGHT

BEYOND THE
SPIRITS BEYOND

On my first visit to the White House, the president and first lady honored me by letting me stay in the Lincoln Bedroom. Retiring to my room, I felt all the thrill of staying in this historical setting: Here Mr. Lincoln had first read aloud the Emancipation Proclamation. The beauty of its Victorian rococo-revival style filled my eyes.

As I studied the copy of the Gettysburg Address, framed and sitting on the desk, the accommodating usher assigned to me knocked on my door. After checking to see that I had everything I needed for the night, he asked, "Have you heard the stories of the appearance of Mr. Lincoln's ghost in this room?" He then detailed some of the over one hundred sightings of the ghost, including one by Queen Elizabeth II!

That story chilled me almost as much as the recent statistic that says 42 percent of all Americans believe they have been in contact with a dead person.[1]

Can the disembodied spirit of President Lincoln still visit the White House? Can the dead come back to haunt us? NO!

Not only has God fixed a great gulf between heaven and hell, one also exists between this life and the afterlife. Jesus' parable of the rich man and poor Lazarus, who begged at the gates, makes that perfectly clear (Luke 16:19–31). Return from the dead simply isn't "policy." What, then, causes sightings such as those in the presidential home?

First, let's admit that such appearances are extraordinarily rare. Though they do take place, and such "persons" have the appearance of the deceased or the voice of a loved one, they do not pop up everywhere.

When such phenomena do occur, they result from one of two sources: trickery or demon manifestation.

Spiritism has a history of trickery. Just as witchcraft includes much that comes from man, spiritism often comes from the deceptions of humans.

For instance Mrs. Blanche Cooler, a medium, supposedly talked to Gordon Davies, who was killed in a war. A voice much like Davies's described unusual features of a house, foretold the future, and shared information unknown to anyone at the séance, ruling out any thought transference. When Davies showed up, alive, a short time later, he was proved to know nothing about the séance.[2] He, like the others, was a victim of her deception.

The rest, the *real,* inexplicable side of mediums and their visions of the future come from demon manifestations. When we seek to explain the knowledge of such beings, we must remember that demons have been around since the dawn of creation. Some have possessed persons who no longer live. Others have heard intimate conversations and know what a human would describe as a "virtually unknown" experience. Though some demons have the power to represent themselves as deceased persons, they *are not* those individuals. We would call them apparitions.

Can the Living Talk to the Dead?

Spiritists claim they can. In 1967 Episcopal bishop James A. Pike brought that idea to the attention of many Americans when he had his séance with Arthur Ford televised. The controversial and colorful bishop *did* have something extraordinary happen to him.

Shortly before his death, Franz Winkler, a German psychiatrist who practiced in New York City, told me the story I now relate. At the time he said he had never told anyone else.

Bishop Pike called Winkler from Los Angeles and

made an appointment. When they met, Pike told Winkler he had been having tremendous personal problems and pressures and had consulted a medium who used hypnosis on him. Under posthypnotic suggestion, the medium informed Pike he could summon Jesus Christ into his presence, and He would physically appear before the bishop.

Persuaded that the posthypnotic suggestion had caused mental strain and stress in Pike's life, Winkler determined the visitations from Christ were hallucinations, but he did not rule out demonic influence in achieving them.

Pike had had a son with whom he did not get along too well, because the boy experimented with LSD, lived for a long time in Haight-Ashbury, and engaged in revolt at Cambridge. In February, 1966, James Pike, Jr., committed suicide.

Bishop Pike traveled to Cambridge, along with his chaplain, David Barr, and his secretary, Maren Bergrud. The three shared a suite in which some strange things happened.

James, Jr., had had some idiosyncrasies, along with his tremendous intellect and personality. Among those idiosyncrasies were a strong dislike for long fingernails and bangs and a love of warm milk and hot rooms.

One morning the bishop awoke in his room in Cambridge to find two of the postal cards his son collected lying on the floor at a 140-degree angle. They marked the time when James, Jr., had died.

When his secretary came into the room, Bishop Pike noted that, much to her chagrin, one-third of her bangs had been trimmed. The next day another third of them had disappeared. On the third night she awoke the others with a scream. Something had been driven beneath the nails of her fingers and two nails had been broken off. When the chaplain and the bishop entered her room, they were startled to see that the rest of her bangs had been trimmed.

In the days that followed, fifty different phenomena occurred in that suite. Items moved; cigarettes no one but James, Jr., had smoked were mysteriously found there. The room temperature changed, and milk delivered fresh that morning soured by noon.

Intrigued, Bishop Pike asked a British minister to get him an appointment with Ena Twigg, one of that nation's foremost mediums. When he visited Twigg, she told him, "He is here and is trying hard to get through to you now." Suddenly her body grew rigid, and a voice with the tonality and inflection of the bishop's son said, "I failed the test, I can't face you, can't face life. I'm confused. Very sudden passing— have had to do this—couldn't find anyone. God, I didn't know what I was doing. But when I got here I found I wasn't such a failure as I thought. My nervous system failed . . . I'm not in purgatory—but something like hell here. Yet nobody blames me here."[3]

In the days that followed, the voice that spoke through Ena Twigg revealed confidential things only a father and son would have known.

Either Bishop Pike had become a victim of one of the world's greatest hoaxes, or Ena Twigg was a real medium with spiritualistic powers that she manifested in a unique way.

Victor Ernest, now a Southern Baptist preacher, at one time had the psychic capacities of levitation and speaking as a medium; he says real communication with the dead cannot occur. Based on his own experiences, he concludes demons can stay so close to a person that they can know his innermost secrets and confidences. By knowing his actions and attitudes and hearing his vocal intonation and inflection, demons may mimic and imitate a human.[4] Ernest says they spoke through him as a medium.

New Age channeling, likewise, does not put a person in touch with the dead. Unlike the messengers of God, such channels do not have a record of always being correct and never contradicting Bible truths. Christians need to treat them as what they really are—prophecies with a demonic origin.

A Look at the Medium

This age of impersonal technology has led to a rise in interest in prophecy. Edgar Cayce, Eileen Garrett, Maurice Woodruff, Criswell, Jesse Stearn, Nostradamus, Jeane Dixon, and Joan Quigley have captured the imagination of millions. These prophets claim to have "looked back" to 18.5 million years ago and "forward" to A.D. 2037.

May 5, 1988, found Joan Quigley out of town. She had prophesied a devastating earthquake in San Francisco that day. Airlines reported a heavier-than-usual flow of traffic the day before, so presumably many had listened to the influential seer. But no quake occurred.

Los Angeles stargazer James Baker foresaw "two major cycles of astrological stress situations between April 23 and May 1." It was supposed to cause a great West Coast quake.[5]

These predictions were allegedly set in motion by a prophecy of the sixteenth-century seer Nostradamus, who reputedly foresaw such events as Napoleon's defeat and the attack on Pearl Harbor. His failure to accurately forecast a great earthquake (supposed to occur in Los Angeles on May 23), would seem to place his other predictions on shaky ground.

The legions of channelers and mediums who have "missed the mark" grows daily. The public hears much about their success, while the media usually ignore the failures. Public image rates higher than the seers' batting average.

Take, for example, Jeane Dixon. When she was eight, her mother took her to see a gypsy woman, and the fortune-teller was impressed by the Star of David with double lines leading from it in the child's left hand and a star on the Mount of Jupiter in the right hand. Later a Hindu mystic confirmed her interpretation that the child had the gift of prophecy. The gypsy gave Jeane her first occult objects. Jeane immediately read the crystal ball and prophesied a forthcoming injury to the gypsy.[6]

But in the January 27, 1968, *Herald News*, she predicted President Lyndon Johnson would be renominated by the Democratic party.[7] Maybe Mr. Johnson had not read the paper when he announced he would not seek reelection, and the Chicago convention gave the nomination to Hubert H. Humphrey.

In the same column, she announced that Mrs. Kennedy was not thinking of remarriage. On October 20, 1968, she claimed her prophecy was still valid. The next day, Jacqueline Kennedy married Aristotle Onassis. Appropriately, the paper inserted a small, bordered statement in Dixon's column, which stated: "Bad day for a seer."

Could This Be Biblical?

How does such prophecy relate to the testimony of Scripture?

It Violates the First Commandment. "Thou shall have no other gods before Me," says God. If an individual allows a medium, gift, or capacity to become more important than the Lord God, he has some other god than Jehovah. Anyone who relies on wisdom other than His places his faith in an inferior product.

King Saul put his faith in the wrong place when he went to consult the witch of En-dor (1 Samuel 28). He had engaged in battle, and things were not going well. Because he had sin in his life, his prayers went unanswered, so Saul looked for another option. In his panic the king instructed his servants to find a woman who had a familiar spirit—a medium—and they sent him to a witch at En-dor.

Saul had such an interest in what the woman had to say that he crossed the battlefield of Armageddon. But when he met with her, she immediately confronted him with his own words. Previously Saul had made a law that anyone who consulted a medium should be put to death. Perhaps she had recognized this man, who stood head and shoulders above the rest (1 Samuel 9:2). At any rate, the witch refused to engage in her art until she had his promise she would not be punished (and who could give that promise but the king?).

The woman saw a vision of an old man covered with a mantle. Neither Saul nor his attendants saw it; only the woman claimed to see a man dressed as one of the prophets of the day, who all wore hooded robes. Saul had asked her to provide Samuel, and *he* decided this was the man she described, though she gave him no identification.

The word used to describe the witch is *ob* in Hebrew. It means "one who speaks from the hollow of the belly," or a ventriloquist. According to the *Davis Dictionary of the Bible* ". . . The voice of the spirit, which appeared to come in a whisper from the ground, emanated from the human pretender himself."[8]

Whoever she saw, it certainly wasn't Samuel.

Saul presented an ideal subject for her kind of manipulation. She no doubt already knew the chances he stood in battle. He was emotionally distraught and incapable of proper leadership. His very presence in her tent proved God no longer controlled his life. When she foretold Saul's death, she really didn't need a nudge from Samuel. Her prophecy became self-fulfilling, since Saul tried to commit suicide on the battlefield.

Christians should know that Satan and the demons cannot predict the future with certainty. They can *only* make "educated guesses." Why break the First Commandment for an educated guess, when you can have the truth from God?

Psychics Are Always Bad News.   Note that psychics almost always predict such events as suicide, murder, war, death, illness, or failure in a business or marriage. Rarely will they tell of something upbeat. When they do, as with Jeane Dixon's prediction of the election, they may also be wrong.

What happened to the good news?

Signs of a True Prophet

Though many mediums and channels may pretend to have a prophetic gift, the Bible describes it in different terms. It says the prophet:

> *Is specifically called to the office by God.* Every prophet in Scripture was called this way. *Never* does the Bible associate a medium with the sacred office.
>
> *Is* never *wrong.* The assertion that many modern-day "prophets" have a 75 percent rate of accuracy thrills many. However, being 75 percent correct looks less

impressive if you consider that they were 25 percent wrong. God cannot be only three-fourths correct. ". . . How shall we know the word which the Lord has not spoken? When a prophet speaks in the name of the Lord, if the thing does not come about or come true, that is the thing which the Lord has not spoken . . ." (*see* Deuteronomy 18:21, 22).

A prophet could not be wrong, because "God cannot lie." Prophetic accuracy is a principle that substantiates the Scripture as the Word of God. Peter asserted that the written Word of God was ". . . a more sure word of prophecy . . ." than eyewitnesses or persons having audibly heard a testimony (2 Peter 1:16–21).

Other Testimony

Not only would faith prohibit involvement with such occult activities, science can support the dangers becoming integrated in the things of Satan may involve. Psychiatrist Dr. George Cox, who has studied in this field, warns that it may result in mediumistic psychosis, depression, melancholy, psychopathic disorders, and severe psychoses.

One therapist described the influence of New Age ideas on normal people, borderlines, and psychotics. Psychologically normal people may seek out the techniques of the New Age to use for their own purposes, and they may show few negative effects, but for the borderline or psychotic individual it could cause serious problems. She warns, "Psychologically speaking, the New Age movement does not herald a new and wondrous era for mankind. Rather it is an arrest in man's development. Morally, emotionally, and spiritually, it is infantile, pathological, and sinful."[9]

If one does not wish to stay away from spiritism for religious reasons, it might still be well to do so for the sake of mental health.

NINE
STAR STRUCK

The crowd wondered curiously why someone had picked 12:10 A.M. for the governor's inauguration. Never before had the taking of the oath of office occurred at such an unorthodox hour.

Only a small, inner circle knew the reason the governor of California would raise his hand to repeat the oath, "I, Ronald Reagan, do solemnly swear . . ." at such a time. The hour had been chosen by a close friend of the governor's wife—an astrologer.

By the time Mrs. Reagan's devotion to astrology hit front-page news, he was president of the United States, and the truth came to light through White House Chief of Staff Donald Regan.

As early as 1950 Mrs. Reagan had dabbled in astrology. In the early part of that decade, Ronald Reagan consulted a horoscope compiled by Caroll Righter as he tried to make a career decision. His 1965 autobiography, *Where's the Rest of Me?* glibly referred to the practice he and Nancy made of checking their horoscopes in a syndicated astrological column. As late as 1980, the year of his election to the presidency, *Newsweek* reported he still checked his horoscope. When the president-elect told a reporter of his consultations with astrologer Jeane Dixon, a delegation from the Federation of American Scientists—which included five Nobel laureates—wrote him, acknowledging this "gravely disturbed" them: "In our opinion, no person whose decisions are based, even in part, on such evident fantasies can be trusted to make the many serious—and even life-and-death—decisions required of American Presidents."[1]

As president, Mr. Reagan's calendar was virtually controlled by the advice of an astrologer, whom *Time* magazine identified as Joan Quigley. According to Donald Regan, the astrologer's influence caused him to keep a color-coded calendar on his desk. Green ink indicated good days, red stood for bad, and yellow meant it was an "iffy" day to move the president from one place to another, schedule a speech, or start negotiations with a foreign power.

In an interview, the former chief of staff said, "It wasn't until it began to impinge and in my judgment harm the presidency in the latter part of 1986 and early 1987 that I began to protest."[2]

At the same time as he used a superstitious

technique—and a demonic one—to direct the country, Ronald Reagan parroted lines that encouraged prayer and endorsed the Bible. He quoted the words his speech writers prepared, while the first lady had her confidante consult the stars.

Carl Gustav Jung observed that astrology "knocks at the doors of the universe from which it was banished 300 years ago."[3] The growth in scientific knowledge had seemed to rid us of idolatry of the planets, but like President and Mrs. Reagan, many people have tried to turn back the clock and resurrect this god of antiquity.

What's Wrong With Astrology?

Whatever astrology is, it isn't a good sign. Like some other occult religions, it is old and has only been recently revived and marketed by keeping its roots covered.

Around 3000 B.C. the Chaldeans and Babylonians began recording observations of the stars. But what began as a primitive science gradually deteriorated to a pseudoscience and then a religion. As the stars began to be regarded as supernatural beings, the civilizations around the Persian Gulf started to worship them.

Eventually this developed into two separate disciplines: natural astrology, known today as astronomy; and judicial astrology, which the Greeks and Romans refined into a system that serves as the basis for today's superstition of astrology.

In spite of having been discredited scientifically,

Chart 3
The Flaws in Astrology

According to Astrology	*According to Science*
The earth is the center of the universe (Ptolemaic system).	Copernicus and Galileo proved the earth revolves around the sun (Copernican system).
The planets known to the ancient peoples influence astrology.	The planets Uranus (1781), Neptune (1846), and Pluto (1930) were discovered after the construction of most astrological charts. Some modern charts give Neptune and Uranus consideration, but Pluto is omitted.[4]
Astrologers use the same zodiac system as the ancient Greeks.	Since Hipparchus (c. 130 B.C.) structured the zodiac, a virtually imperceptible shift has occurred in the line of the poles, called the procession of the equinoxes. Each has shifted approximately one month, so Aries is now Taurus, Taurus is Gemini, and so on. This distorts both the charts and the philosophy behind them.[5]

No planet or sign of the zodiac is visible north of the Arctic Circle for several weeks.	Anyone born in Alaska, Canada, Finland, Greenland, Norway, Siberia, Sweden, or in other Arctic areas cannot have a valid horoscope.[6]
The number of houses (constellations) comprising the zodiac belt varies, depending on the school of astrology. Some say there are eight, some ten, most claim there are twelve, but numbers go as high as twenty-four.	This is a wide, variable base on which to establish a "science."
No one is able to accurately determine the precise date of a new star age. The beginning of the Age of Aquarius has been given dates as varied as 1904, 1910, 1917, 1936, 1962, 2160, 2375, and 3000.[7]	Why can't a "science" determine anything as basic as this?
Astrology alleges the rays of the planets that fall upon a child at birth are a decisive influence in his life.	Planets emit no light of their own. Fixed stars are the source of light, and the Milky Way is the source of cosmic rays. All other planets, like Earth, emit neither light nor cosmic rays.

especially by astronomy (*see* Chart 3), the old religion of astrology now enjoys popularity. One estimate says approximately 10,000 persons work full-time in it. Nearly 200,000 work in it part-time.[8] Over three-fourths of the country's daily newspapers carry horoscopes. Twenty-three percent of Americans believe in astrology.[9]

Masses of people search their horoscopes daily to find meaning to life. British astrological historian Louis MacNeice confesses "curiosity about the future is a primary reason for the continuing popularity of astrology."[10]

In addition, the almost cozy appeal of fatalism attracts people. During times of stress or failure, the stars can provide a cop-out. By believing "it's all in the stars," one need not accept personal blame.

Others derive delight from astrology's classification system that allows them to identify with persons of notoriety, prominence, and success. Sharing a sign with someone seems to bring its own feeling of closeness and importance.

Then How Can It Work?

If astrology has such a false base, how can it seem to "work" for so many people? I would like to suggest that two factors relate to its success.

Astrology Is a Form of Idolatry. Those who look to the stars for guidance treat them as idols when they see the heavenly bodies as superior beings that control destiny.

Paul warned that the idol is nothing; however, behind each idol lies a working host of demons (1 Corinthians 10:19–21). Such spirits may influence the affairs of the idolater, to divert his attention from the God who "telleth the number of the stars and calleth them all by their names" (*see* Psalms 147:4). (When you consider that if you counted one of the stars in the Andromeda Galaxy each second since the birth of Christ, you would have counted less than a third of its total, that's some feat![11])

It Becomes a Self-Fulfilling Prophecy. Tests have proven that athletes fumble because they think *fumble*. Many persons who cause accidents "always thought it would happen."

Maxwell Maltz says of such image fulfillment:

There is an abundance of scientific evidence which shows that the human brain and nervous system operate purposefully in accordance with the known principles of Cybernetics to accomplish goals of the individual. Insofar as function is concerned, the brain and nervous system constitute a marvelous and complex "goal-striving mechanism," a sort of built-in automatic guidance system which works for you as a "success mechanism" or against you as a "failure mechanism," depending on how "YOU," the operator, operate it and the goals you set for it.[12]

Astrologers make the most of this principle. Once they give him an idea, the person who has become involved in astrology may well only have to rely on his own mind to make it happen.

In addition, note how many astrology predictions are so broad that they could fit just about any situation. Such vagueness helps improve the likelihood that an individual will find this "truth" in her life.

Scripture reminds us that "as a man thinketh so is he" (*see* Proverbs 23:7). A person with any degree of superstition, instability, or desire to have astrology prove true may see it happen, just the way a child who wants to fulfill his parents' wishes may live out their descriptions of him. If they say Johnny is good, he may become a prize student, but if they have no use for him, he may become the worst kid on the block to prove that they are right.

I have recorded numerous instances in which a person was given the wrong horoscope for a given day and told it was her own. Believing it, she would later report it had been fulfilled on that day. The power of suggestion is very great.

More Testimony Against Astrology

The Word of Scripture

Astrology comes from two Greek words, *astra*, meaning "stars," and *logos*, meaning "word, logic, or reason." Together the two mean "word of the stars."

Concerning these two Greek words the Bible has something else to say. In the introduction to his gospel, John reminds us that before time began the *logos* was. In this context he refers to Jesus Christ. Before the stars were strewn in the heavens, Jesus was "the bright and morning star" (Revelation 22:16). The Word of God, the bright and morning star, often conflicts with the word of the stars. Any attempt to wed astrology and Christianity results in a fraudulent relationship.

The Bible, especially the Old Testament, speaks out against astrology and the worship of the planets (*see* Chart 4). Instead of becoming involved in such things, the believer does well to seek Him "who makes the Pleiades and Orion, who turns blackness to morning and darkens day to night" (*see* Amos 5:8). The Creator, not His resplendent creation, should be the object of our adoration.

What About the Advent Star? Does the Bible ever seem to speak favorably about astrology? Some claim that the star of Bethlehem endorses it.

The word *magi* originally referred to Medes who served as Zoroastrian priests for the Persians. Later the title described magicians in general, regardless of their nationality. According to William Smith, "The religion of Zoroaster . . . preserved the hope of a great deliverer, who should reform the world, and establish a reign of universal peace. That some tradition, influenced possibly by the Jews of the dispersion, went so far as to make

Chart 4
Astrology and Scripture

Biblical Reference	Injunction
Deuteronomy 18:10–12	All occult practices are forbidden by God. Those who engaged in them should be driven out.
2 Kings 23:3–5	King Josiah makes a covenant with God to follow Him. He removes the idolatrous priests from the land, "them also that burned incense unto Baal, to the sun, and to the moon, and to the planets, and to all the host of heaven."
Isaiah 47:13, 14	Isaiah mocked the futility of the astrologers to help the children of Israel.
Daniel 2:2–47	Daniel revealed the fakery and futility of the arts of the astrologers, magicians, and soothsayers of Babylon.
Amos 5	Historically the god Moloch had planetary and solar associations. Amos condemned such worship, which involved infant sacrifice and prostitution.
Jeremiah 10:2, 3, 7	Jeremiah warned against all heathen practices (idolatry) and encouraged the people to trust God instead of the "wise men" of other nations.

this deliverer a 'king of the Jews,' seems a fair inference from the direct form of their inquiry for Him."[13]

The magi are the only star watchers referred to favorably in the Bible, and the star was extraterrestrial, used by God to identify His Son to men. The events were not meant to glorify the method God used to bring men to Him, but to glorify the One identified by them.

The Word of Astrology Charting

Not only does Scripture provide reasons not to engage in this occult phenomenon, astrology speaks against itself. Though many people may follow it and even swear by it, it has a high failure rate. Perhaps that's why so many syndicated astrological columns take refuge in vague predictions one finds hard to prove or disprove. I compared four syndicated articles, using the birthdate of March 7 as my base. Here's what I found.

Three out of four did mention finances. One linked it to a change in attitude, which would increase earnings and predicted an agreement that could mean thousands of dollars. Another told the reader he had acumen, but needed to go for a more creative career. The third merely encouraged efforts concerning job and financial opportunities.

Two predicted a new maturity, but one vaguely spoke of benefits, while the other linked it to a job.

Concerning relationships, one spoke of a relationship that turned a corner; the second described a dislike for subordinate positions and recommended a partnership; while the third predicted a desire for children and a spirit of romance that would mold a relationship. The fourth horoscope dealt almost entirely with relationships, describing the reader as one who appeared vulnerable but had great strength. He also had great faith in people and many friends.

Other topics mentioned included psychic impressions, confidence, intuition, musical talent, ideals, wearing bright colors, and social opportunities. Hard to believe something in that smattering of concepts could not hit home for everyone!

Even if you pay more than the cost of a newspaper and get a personal reading, the many sources used by astrologers guarantee that if you do not like your first chart, you can go to someone else who will provide something different.

Dependability is not astrology's middle name!

The Word of Scientific Testing

In one of the earliest and most exhaustive scientific tests of astrology, Europeans Michael and Francois Gauquelin assembled and studied the horoscopes of over 25,000 persons. (European birth certificates indicate the time of birth, which allows those writing up horoscopes to do them more "accurately.")

Their conclusions? Michael Gauquelin wrote: "It is now quite certain that the signs in the sky which presided over births have no power whatever to decide our fates, to affect our hereditary characteristics, or to play any part, however humble, in the totality of effects, random or otherwise, which form the fabric of our lives and mold our impulses to actions."[14]

As if that left any doubt about his educated convictions, he also stated: "Every effort made by astrologers to defend their basic postulate, that the movement of the stars can predict destiny has failed. . . . Statistics have disposed of old arguments once and for all: the numbers speak without bias, and they leave no room for doubt. Whoever claims to predict the future by consulting the stars is fooling either himself or someone else."[15]

Logically, some have argued that if the stars have any influence on a person, his horoscope should be based on the hour of conception, not birth. At conception, genetic makeup programs such elements as sex, race, physical traits, and even personality and behavior. But that would make natal charts incorrect by about nine months, and how many conceptions can anyone identify that exactly?

Even the best astrologers have problems making up something acceptable by scientists. In the December, 1985, issue of *Nature* magazine, Shawn Carlson, a physicist at Lawrence Berkeley Laboratories reported on "a doubleblind test of astrology" he conducted along with other scientists. Enlisting the aid of the National Council for Geocosmic Research, they got twenty-eight reputable chart makers to take part in an extensive test, using an objective pool of two hundred volunteers who had neither had their astrological charts made before nor strongly disbelieved in astrology. Of the conclusive results of the test, Carlson commented:

> We bent over backwards to find astrologers who were respected by other astrologers. We explicitly wanted people who were held in high esteem by their peers— giving them every chance for success.
>
> We are now in a position to argue a surprisingly strong case against natal astrology as practiced by reputable astrologers. Great pains were taken to insure that the experiment was unbiased and to make sure that astrology was given every reasonable chance to succeed. It failed.
>
> After all the studies that have been done on astrology, anyone who spends more time on it has to be a fool. No study has ever shown that astrology has any effect. No hint of an effect. The issue is settled.[16]

PART III
THE CONQUERED LION

---------- TEN ----------

REACHING OUT
TO A NEW AGE

No matter how much we might think otherwise,
America is a religious nation. According to Roger Ellwood:

> Americans expect much from religion. Foreign observ-
> ers often insist that America is the most religious nation
> in the world. If so (and of course no generalization of
> this sort means much) it is not because America is tied to
> traditional religion to the same extent some Asian
> nations still are, but because Americans—unlike mod-
> ernized people in some other countries—seem unable to
> become completely and happily secular. Even while

147

expect religion to produce happiness, they set up poles of time and place as sacred, they feel religious guilt, they use religion as justification for everything from national policy to individual vocation, they look for it to handle personal disappointments and sorrows. In terms of expectation, America is perhaps a very religious country. For this reason it will continue to be a very creative country religiously.[1]

The only question now is what direction is that creativity going in? A large part of it *has* turned from Christianity, often from an emotionally cold and theologically dull religion that has not seemed to answer questions. Many persons have seen through the guise of nominal Christianity or have given up on a Christian faith they believe has "failed." Their search for more may have led them away from Christ.

One author points out the subtle change that has come over America in the past years:

> The Judeo-Christian heritage may officially sanction society's institutions, but its concepts of God and reality rooted in objective revelation mean little to the average person. The world-view held by most is subtly embedded with a distinctly Eastern mode of interpreting man's relationship to God and the material universe. America's monetary system proclaims, "In God We Trust," but its spiritual consciousness bears the inscription, "Mystery Babylon."[2]

Can we blame people who have turned away from a meaningless Christianity that held nothing of the power of God? For many have had contact only with something that called itself Christian—but it has known nothing of Christ. A smaller number may have grown up in homes where Christ *was* known, but they have not personally accepted Him. And some Christians, new to the faith and unfamiliar with its teachings, may have been lured into a New Age group that sounded right. Even those who have been in the faith for a long time, but find appeal in its teachings, may discover some fulfillment of desire in a New Age.

Attractions of a New Age

Most evangelicals, asked to pick a New Age proponent out of a lineup, would seek out the most wild-eyed and ill-dressed person in the bunch. But in so doing, they would miss out on most New Agers. The typical New Ager is an average, normal-looking person in search of a better life.

Younger adherents of New Age groups frequently come from unstable families, but not always. Just as often, they are pseudointellectuals, frustrated by their own sense of powerlessness and meaninglessness.

Adult adherents often enter the door into New Age while going through personal trauma. During a time of bereavement, a widow may turn to channeling and spiritualism; the loss of a job may prompt a young man to investigate TM; a divorce or a painful rejection may cause a young woman to play around with witchcraft or some other form of the occult.

In short, most people who get involved in the New Age do so because they have big needs and do not see conventional answers.

Others, however, get involved simply because it seems to be the "in" thing to do. It appears attractive and exciting, and it seems to explore a world that they have not previously investigated. As they explore, they see some mysterious things happen that they can't explain, and they are hooked.

It is all quite understandable. With all the family, economic, ecological, and social problems man faces today, it's easy to feel intimidated. New Age movements promise solutions that transcend the world.

Sharing the Gospel in a New Age

Because most New Age persons seek solutions that transcend the world, Christians will not have trouble finding an opening to present the gospel. The problem is, many New Agers are already familiar with a "gospel" that has never transcended this world.

In addition, there are other difficulties in witnessing to New Agers. As they witness, Christians should ask these questions:

1. *What does the Bible say?*
    To understand the mechanics of what goes on in witnessing, the Christian will need to know both what the Bible says and what the New Agers believe. Before witnessing, Christians should be able to speak

clearly about the gospel and know what concepts do not agree with it.

2. *What are New Agers looking for?*

People become involved with the New Age because they search for something. As they talk with these seekers, Christians should discover what specific benefits New Age proponents wish to receive. What chance does one have of finding them in the New Age? What does the Bible teach concerning these things?

3. *What do the words mean?*

New Age groups have their own vocabulary, and some words familiar to Christians have different meanings for New Agers. Awareness of the ideas behind the words will improve communication between the Christian and New Age believer.

4. *What does this New Age group teach?*

Various elements of the movement differ (*see* Chart 5 for general New Age beliefs and how they compare with Christianity). By discovering specific beliefs, the Christian can reach out more effectively. This will require asking questions, prayerfully reading up on the beliefs of a group, and active searching of the Scripture.

5. *How do New Agers understand Christianity?*

Many New Age persons have misconceptions about Christianity. During conversation, these need to be discovered and true concepts explained.

6. *Is it clear this is not an attack?*

Those who witness to New Age proponents should not seek to destroy the worldview of the New Age—though it is very different from the Christian one. Instead, they should present Christ's message in love.

151

Chart 5
New Age Versus Christian Beliefs

Because New Age beliefs vary so much from one group to another, all the concepts below may not apply to one group, but most have at least some of these in common.

New Age	Christianity	Scriptural Support
God cannot be known personally. God is too cosmic, a "life force."	Humans can know God as individuals, in an intimate fashion.	John 3:16; Psalm 139
Man is god.	Man is a sinful human being, created by God.	Romans 3:23; Genesis 1:27
Sin does not exist; evil comes because man wishes it upon himself.	Sin has broken man's relationship with God, but Christ reconciles man to Him.	Romans 1:18; 3:23–26; 2 Corinthians 5:16
Man has no need for salvation; he needs enlightenment.	Man *must* have salvation through Christ.	John 3:16–21
Enlightenment will provide perfection for man.	Perfection only comes through faith in Christ.	Hebrews 13:20, 21
Many groups believe ultimate oneness may be achieved through reincarnation.	Christ provides one-time forgiveness.	Romans 5:18, 19; 1 John 1:9

People must seek to transform themselves by acts.	People must seek regeneration in Christ. Our actions can show we know Him.	Romans 6:8–11; Colossians 3:10; 1 John 2:1–5
Man is relatively unimportant in this universe.	Man is important to God.	Psalms 31:23, 24; 139
Nothing on earth is real.	Earthly existence is real but temporary. There also are eternal realities.	Genesis 1; 2 Corinthians 4:18
People must seek to become "one" with the universe.	People must seek personal closeness with God.	James 4:8; Psalm 63
People must seek a new state of consciousness.	People should walk after the spirit of Christ.	Romans 8:1, 2
Tolerant of many truths and is somewhat antiscientific.	One truth exists and world reality reflects this.	John 14:6; Romans 1:19–21
Seeks to reconcile man with despair.	Seeks to bring man to joy in Christ.	Romans 14:17
Promises an earthly New Age of peace and perfection.	Promises God's peace on earth and an eternal heavenly perfection.	Romans 5:1; 8:6; 2 Corinthians 5:1; 1 Peter 5:10

7. *Have the issues been identified and addressed?*

New Age adherents may appear to agree with so much of what Christians affirm that it may seem as if they were Christians themselves. New Age movements are often inclusive and will try to accept much of Christianity under their nebulous umbrella. Christianity states that Jesus Christ is the unique Son of God and is the only Way.

8. *Is this faith that touches the heart and mind?*

Many New Age members have not seen both the experiential and intellectual sides of Christianity. They consider it a rational, empty religion. Showing both sides should become part of effective witnessing.

9. *How much time will it take?*

Because New Age thinking differs so greatly from Christianity, Christians should not expect overnight changes. Evangelism in the New Age may take time.

10. *Has the hope of Christ been adequately portrayed?*

The ultimate emptiness of the New Age may finally cause a person to turn from it. The Beatles, who did much to popularize Maharishi Mahesh Yogi and Transcendental Meditation, spoke glowingly of him at first; but in a few years they became disenchanted.[3] The hope of the gospel can say much to those who seek a way out of the New Age.

Caring communication of the gospel leads individuals to faith in Christ. It is no less the Christian's responsibility to reach out to members of the New Age than to anyone else.

———————— ELEVEN ————————

RESISTING THE DEVIL

"Resist the devil," Scripture commands, "and he will flee from you" (*see* 1 Peter 5:8, 9). But how can Christians do that?

To begin, we need to prepare ourselves for the spiritual battle by knowing our enemy and the weapons and defenses God has planned for us.

The Enemy We Face

As Christians we should not fool ourselves into thinking of Satan as a weak, spineless being who can have no influence over us. His very real power has the ability to:

> Subtlely influence us (Genesis 3:1)
> Provoke us (1 Chronicles 21:1)
> Rob us (Luke 8:12)
> Hinder us (1 Thessalonians 2:18)
> Persecute us (2 Corinthians 12:7)

Like the lion Scripture calls him, Satan has sharp claws that can cause the unwary much harm.

Satan's Weapons

Satan uses three weapons against humans:

> *Oppression.* He may work in a person's life without his knowing it. By bringing influences to bear on an individual's life, the devil encourages him to resist good and advocate evil. Depression, despondency, and even a desire to kill himself may show up in that person's life.
>
> *Obsession.* A person may so dwell on Satan and the occult that he becomes preoccupied with it and diverted from God's will. He may experience the same emotional problems the oppressed person encounters.
>
> *Possession.* A person may knowingly enter into league with Satan and allow demons to inhabit his body. When Jesus met the man on the shores of the Sea of Galilee, so many demons filled him that they named themselves "Legion." Possession opens a person to more than one demonic influence.

The way Satan uses these weapons depends on whom he attacks. Because the non-Christian does not have the Spirit of Christ to protect and fill him, he can experience all three. Though not all non-Christians go as far as possession, they are under Satan's mastery and have no power to keep him at bay.

The Christian cannot experience possession, because the Spirit of Christ has control of his life. However, oppression and obsession may still influence him if he does not take steps against them.

Defense for the Non-Christian. To combat demonization, the non-Christian must come to know Christ. He needs to consider his spiritual condition by asking four questions and understanding the scriptural answers to them:

1. *Who has sinned?*
"For all have sinned, and come short of the glory of God" (Romans 3:23).
2. *What is the penalty for sin?*
"The wages of sin is death; but the gift of God is eternal life through Jesus Christ our Lord" (Romans 6:23).
3. *How may I be saved?*
"That if thou shalt confess with thy mouth the Lord Jesus, and shalt believe in thine heart that God hath raised him from the dead, thou shalt be saved. For with the heart man believeth unto righteousness; and with the mouth confession is made unto salvation" (Romans 10:9, 10).
"For whosoever shall call upon the name of the Lord shall be saved" (Romans 10:13).

4. *What happens when I ask Christ to save me?*

"Behold, I stand at the door and knock: if any man hear my voice, and open the door, I will come in to him, and will sup with him, and he with me" (Revelation 3:20).

Battling the devil begins with knowing Christ. Apart from Him, there is no victory.

Defense for the Christian. Those who are new to Christ and have been involved with the occult need to confess their involvement and turn aside from it as did the new Christians in Acts 19:17–20. If they have been involved in drug use, they need to realize this ally of the occult may still influence their bodies. By asking the Lord Jesus to rid them of all lingering effects, they may receive freedom from such bondage.

Satan cannot possess the Christian, but 2 Corinthians 11:4 says a Christian may be confronted by those who offer another spirit—a satanic one—and it can have some power over him. If this has happened, he needs to take three steps:

1. He should renounce his interest in the occult. Most people think of sins in terms of adultery, murder, and so on. They may not add to that list palm reading, astrology, fortune-telling, witchcraft, satanism, or any other black arts, but God does. Like any other sins, the occult ones must be brought before Him.

2. Personal cleansing should be obtained through the practice of 1 John 1:9, "If we confess our sins, he is

faithful and just to forgive us our sins, and to cleanse us from all unrighteousness."

3. He should practice forgiveness of others, as Matthew 6:15 instructs, "But if ye forgive not men their trespasses, neither will your Father forgive your trespasses." The unforgiving are unforgiven because they are unforgivable.

The Christian who has appropriated God's forgiveness needs to become filled with the Spirit, which simply means allowing God to lead, master, control, protect, and preserve his life. When he accepted Christ, the believer became baptized with the Spirit. That means he became identified with Christ through the Spirit. Scripture clearly describes a second act, a filling, in which the believer constantly walks with Him.

Resisting Satan requires both filling and baptism. Only those who have experienced both will fight effectively for God.

Activating a System of Defense

Acknowledging the influence Satan may have on lives, Alan Reed, Jr., a Milwaukee psychiatrist, says one should not rule out possession as an explanation of extreme psychic disorders: "In the whole field of spiritualism, mysticism, religion, and the human spirit, there are things so minimally understood that almost anything's possible."[1] Dr. Walter Brown, a psychiatrist at Mt. Sinai Hospital, in New York City, observed, "In a way, all psychoanalysis and psychotherapy are forms of exorcism, getting rid of demons."[2] No matter what it has been called, throughout the ages mankind has sought release from the demonic. When psychology seeks to fight alone, it can only access the limited resources of the world; it does not realize the power of Christ. For the Christian, it need not stop there.

Begin With Jesus. When we fight Satan, we do not go into battle alone. Though we wrestle against ". . . principalities, against powers, against the rulers of the darkness of this world, against the spiritual wickedness in high places" (Ephesians 6:12), we do not go into the match by ourselves. We go in the power of Jesus, who:

> Came to destroy the works of Satan (1 John 3:8).
> Triumphed over the forces of evil (Colossians 2:15).
> Brought to naught the power of sin (Hebrews 2:14, 15).
> Came to set the captive free (Luke 4:18).

We need to rely on those spiritual facts for our support in battle. With our feet set firmly on the solid Rock, we can ready ourselves for battle.

Take Preventative Action. To prepare for battle, the Christian should take these steps:

1. *Not love Satan, but respect him.*
   Even the angel Michael dared not rebuke Satan, but left that to God (Zechariah 3:2). Christians must respect

160

the devil's capacity for cunning but not confront him on their own. He took on Peter, Judas, Barnabas, and Paul and won. No Christian should take him lightly.

2. *Know how he operates.*

Satan picks his moments and uses subtle tactics. Often he will slip in after a Christian has just experienced a great spiritual victory. Immediately after His baptism, Satan tempted Christ. Can we expect less?

3. *Establish a positive, Bible-based thought pattern regarding demons.*

Instead of becoming preoccupied with Satan, the Christian should focus on Jesus and His love.

By studying God's Word, the believer becomes closer to Him and ready to repulse attack. Christ defeated Satan with Scripture as He responded, "Get behind Me, Satan! For it is written. . ." (Luke 4:8 NKJV). A Christian can also resist him with the Word. He need not worry, because God "has not given . . . a spirit of fear" (2 Timothy 1:7 NKJV). As long as the believer rests in Him, She will have God's protection.

4. *Develop a life-style that recognizes and avoids the tempter.*

No single spiritual experience will permanently immunize the Christian from temptations and problems. He must continually: (a) recognize Satan as the source of temptation (James 1:13). (b) Yield his body to the Lord (Romans 12:1, 2). (c) Exercise his will to walk in Christ (Colossians 2:6). (d) Refuse to obey fleshly desires (Romans 6:12). (e) Abstain from the practice of sin (Romans 6:13). (f) Not give place to the devil (Ephesians 4:27).

Every Christian should also avoid flirting with even the most elemental form of the occult. By avoiding all evil—even the appearance of it—one becomes a better soldier for God.

5. *Cultivate spiritual mechanisms for fleeing the tempter.*

God always provides a way out of temptation. However, the Christian has the responsibility to precommit himself to looking for that way out. By deciding ahead of time, he increases his chances of making the right move in the heat of battle. Leaving it for the last moment may only prepare him for defeat.

6. *Employ the power of prayer and praise.*

To use these powerful weapons the Christian must: (a) Realize holiness is essential in prayer (1 Timothy 2:8). (b) Pray as Christ's proxy (John 14:14). (c) Make prayer a daily practice (Ephesians 6:18). (d) Pray for deliverance from temptation (Matthew 6:13). (e) Express gratitude to the Lord (Philippians 4:6).

Taking up Arms

Just as a soldier trains with arms, the Christian must ready himself for spiritual battle. He must wear the right clothing and perfect his maneuvers, preparing for a sudden attack, because the devil does not give warning of his coming. Anyone wielding a rusty sword and covering himself with a smashed-in helmet cannot effectively fight. If his sandals don't fit, he cannot defend himself on stony ground.

In Ephesians 6:11–18 Paul describes the Christian's battle equipment. With these he can fend off attack and deal the devil a powerful blow:

Truth. When Jesus spoke of the devil, He said, ". . . When he speaketh a lie, he speaketh of his own: for he is a liar, and the father of it" (John 8:44). Lies are a part of Satan's nature—and the natures of those who follow him. We need to stand against them with the truth.

162

Jesus always confronted Satan with Scripture. We gird our loins with the same weapon (Ephesians 6:14).

Righteousness. Paul says we protect our chests with the breastplate of righteousness.

Proverbs 11:3–8 compares the benefits and protection God confers on the righteous to the punishment He promises for the wicked. As we live righteously, we gain power against Satan.

Gospel of peace. In the middle of battle, we have the *gospel*, the "good news," of peace with God (v. 15). While those who do not know Him search endlessly for peace on earth, in the midst of Satan's worst attacks we know we can rest in our relationship with Him (Romans 5:1). Paul says we stand on this, when he says our feet are shod with the gospel of peace (v. 15).

Faith. The shield of faith protects us from the darts of the wicked (v. 16). By faith we know Jesus and have acquired peace with Him (Romans 5:1). Without it, what do we have?

Salvation. We wear salvation on our heads, as helmets (v. 17). Faith allows us to appropriate the salvation God provides in Christ Jesus. Knowing Him as Lord protects our minds, keeping us from the confusion Satan would pour out on us. First Thessalonians 5:8 also adjures the Christian to put on "for an helmet, the hope of salvation."

The sword of the Spirit. All the other elements Paul described were for the Christian's protection. Now he describes the method of attack (v. 17). The sword is the Word of God. By attacking on our own, we fail. Only with the strength of His Word can we successfully combat Satan.

Notice, though, that we cannot decide we simply don't feel like wearing that heavy helmet or don't think the style of the footwear is fashionable. We have to "put on the whole armor of God . . ." in order to stand (v. 11). Through what God has provided for us, we have the proper tools for the job, but we can't try to become commanders who redesign the defense system. We go into battle wearing what God provides, or we don't go in at all.

Defeat of the Enemy

When dealing with evil spirits, Christians should do so in union with Jesus Christ. According to 1 Corinthians 1:30, that's what believers have. Confidence in the ability to do battle does not rest with them, but with the work of Jesus. He has already taken on Satan one-on-one and come out a winner. He has:

> Already triumphed over evil forces (Colossians 2:15).
> Destroyed the works of Satan (1 John 3:8).
> Overcome all satanic power and energy by becoming the sacrificial Lamb (Revelation 12:11).

Those who remain identified with Jesus can appropriate His power.

Who Is Really Winning? What does appropriating His power mean? Can we rely on it? If Christ has already won, why does the battle still seem to rage?

Second Timothy 3:1, 2 describes the last days, saying, "This know also, that in the last days perilous times shall come. For men shall be lovers of their own selves, covetous, boasters, proud, blasphemers, disobedient to parents, unthankful, unholy." As in the time of Christ, demonic activity seems to be breaking forth with increased fervor. Newspapers, periodicals, and the electronic media focus on it—often favorably. We see news reports of psychics who have helped solve crimes, magazine articles that purport to help expand one's abilities through meditation or some occult art, movies that are actively satanic and appeal to youth. At times the devil seems to hold all the cards.

As the Second Coming draws nearer, Satan increases his attacks. Although he cannot avoid the lake of fire God has prepared for him and his followers, the devil seeks to do as much damage as possible in the time he has left.

Can Satan's continued influence prove that Jesus' death was ineffectual? Never! What may seem defeat for God has another purpose. "The Lord is slow to anger, and great in power, and will not at all acquit the wicked . . ." (Nahum 1:3). "The Lord is not slack concerning his promise, as some men count slackness; but is longsuffering to us-ward, not willing that any should perish, but that all should come to repentance" (2 Peter 3:9). As we wait for the closing of this age, let us keep His promises in mind!

TWELVE

CAN IT STRIKE CLOSE TO HOME?

We'd like to think that, as Christians, we're automatically armored against the occult and New Age influences that eddy around us. But as one expert on the New Age testifies:

> A worried churchgoer tells me about a pastor of a local evangelical church who is becoming increasingly involved in New Age literature and seminars, all the while convincing most of his congregation that all is well. Last year I helped a local pastor get his Christian daughter out of a New Age cult. Children are often exposed to New Age ideas and practices in public schools.[1]

It is all around us, and we can't count on some sort of magical defense against the attacks of Satan. For us it is a battle, and we may not like to take a place on the front line, but when that's where God calls us, we must go.

Who Gets Involved?

Do the people who become involved in such groups simply have no contact with Christianity? No. Many come from at least a nominal Christian background. Edgar Cayce, founder of the cultic Association for Research and Enlightenment, Inc., was a student of the Bible, an active church member, and Sunday-school teacher. Jim Jones and Sun Myung Moon both had more traditional church backgrounds before they founded their cults. Selena Fox, a high priestess of witchcraft, was raised as a Baptist.[2]

Having had a conventional Christian background does not preserve one from the influence of Satan. If people do not see some results from their faith, they will probably turn away. "When people see things going wrong all around them and begin asking whether God is all that powerful, people turn to satanism," warns author Ted Schwartz. "When there's a sense of being overwhelmed, people turn to satanism."[3] You could probably say the same thing about those who seek out any other group in the New Age or occult movements.

Sometimes even Christians become involved in New

Age or cultic ideas. In many cases, young Christians who have not yet gotten a deep background in the Bible and knowledge of what it means to be a Christian will fall into the trap of someone who appears acceptable but has diverted from the faith. But it can also happen to older, more experienced Christians. So many groups or ideas *sound* good—at first hearing.

Avoiding the Trap

The world outside it can begin to influence the church, too. Concepts from the New Age or the occult will come into contact with evangelical believers and may even make their way into Christian thinking. How can we recognize the devil's subtle ploys?

First, we need to look at the ultimate thinking behind terminology. Often the New Age or occult appeals to Christianity by using its own words. "My mission," claimed Sun Myung Moon, "is to try to unite all Christians into one family before the Lord arrives."[4] His Presbyterian and Pentecostal background may have given him the terminology, but from the beginning, Moon's cultic church that denies the effectiveness of Jesus' sacrifice and uses many New Age and occult concepts has drawn controversy. Calling his organization the Unification Church and using the name of Christ cannot make it Christian.

Next we must compare any group's or individual's teachings with Scripture. Those who include anything extrabiblical or twist Scripture must be discovered and confuted.

When a teacher seeks to have full control of followers' thoughts and actions, we need to beware. Totally revering one person is dangerous, and cults frequently become established around one charismatic figure, whose words become a curious gospel.

We also need to treat carefully any group that shows an exclusive, superior attitude toward its way to God. Many cults require members to adhere to specific rules and claim to have the only path to Him. Unlike the numerous denominations in Christianity, which may "agree to disagree in love" over some practices, they will remain adamant about beliefs. While the Christian community focuses on Christ and allows some minor differences in practice, cults will demand one specific way in order to receive salvation.

Before we can combat wrong teachings, we need to know Scripture and use it properly. Luke commended the Bereans for checking the teachings of Paul and Silas with God's Word (Acts 17:10, 11), and obviously they knew their Bibles well. Like them, we need to make regular devotions and Bible study part of our lives. In addition, we may want to read up on the groups that belong to the New Age or occult, so that we can witness to those involved in them. But in everything, we need to do so prayerfully and be aware of the deceptiveness of the teachings we deal with.

Once we have become aware of the concepts of our faith and those that do not align with it, we need to share them with our families and church communities. Keeping them to ourselves prevents them from helping others.

Protecting Our Children

In the seventies many cults and New Age groups focused on young people. Because they were facing some important points in their lives, making decisions that might seem beyond them, youth became particularly susceptible to the lure of promises for a happy life and eternity. Though many groups have now expanded to older folks, too, we cannot use that as an excuse not to let our children know what they may face at school, in the workplace, and among friends.

Journalists Carroll Stoner and Jo Anne Parke researched what made young people join cults. To their surprise, they discovered that many came from seemingly normal home lives. But the pattern of those who avoided cults was made up of "honest parents with strong value systems . . . who are willing to work hard to do what they believe is right, people who can honestly face their emotions and their instincts and each other, and are not afraid to confront their children."[5]

Lest that should seem impossible, let's look at a few ways we can make it happen.

Provide a Real Faith. By making certain we live at home as active Christians, we increase the possibility that our children will accept Christ. In addition, youth will need an active church, with a good group for their own age. By providing models and friends who share their faith, we can increase the opportunities for youngsters to have a deeper Christian life.

Teach the Doctrines of Faith. By helping them understand the Bible and the basic doctrines of Christianity, we give children a secure foundation on which to build their own beliefs and a weapon with which to counteract false teachings. Regular teaching in church and Sunday school should be supplemented with teaching in the home. A family that encourages devotions and Bible reading, along with a personal walk that pleases Christ, can better withstand the deceptions of a New Age.

Teach the Realities of Life. Many youngsters have grown up with the idea that everything has a simple answer and that life will always be easy. When confronted with tough times, they become confused and open to the attacks of New Age or occult groups. By providing stable values that do not place too much emphasis on immediate gratification, financial success, or easy answers, we provide children with a defense against trouble. As they combine this with faith in Christ, they will have a firm base to stand on.

Provide a Secure Family Life. Children need parents who sincerely and freely care for them and show it. Both the overly protective and the unloving parent can cause a child to feel insecure and seek out another option in faith. Emotional warmth and stability in the family create a loving bond that can protect a child from a feeling of hopelessness when she faces problems.

Build Self-Esteem in a Child. Loving relationships that show him he is accepted as he is will give a child a sense of safety. By showing him he is valuable, parents increase a child's positive feelings about himself.

Provide a Warm Church Life. As children feel acceptance and love in the Christian community, they will learn that knowing God means more than mouthing certain creeds. If they feel warmth from a larger community, it will reinforce the knowledge gained in the family.

When difficult times come, children need to know they can count on the church for backing. As others reach out to them in love, they will experience a closeness that will encourage them in a Christian way of life.

Encourage Discernment and Thought. As children learn to discern truth from lies and weigh the alternatives in their actions, they build a defense against those who would draw them from Christ. Faith that follows blindly is easily led to a dead end.

Even within the church, the child should learn to discern doubtful teachings from accurate ones. Though we may see more New Age influence outside the church, it does not stop at any building's doors.

Discourage Drug Use. Many occult groups rely heavily on drugs to reach another level of consciousness. By removing that as an option, we protect our children from both physical and spiritual harm.

"Behold," Jesus warned us, "I send you forth as sheep in the midst of wolves: be ye therefore wise as serpents, and harmless as doves" (Matthew 10:16). As we face the New Age and occult, we need to prepare ourselves for conflict, but we can win the ultimate victory in Christ. By making our families and churches aware of the beliefs and groups that threaten, we can begin to resist the lion and have victory—in Him.

APPENDIX
RESOURCES

Organizations

For more specific information on individual groups, you may wish to contact some of the organizations that provide resources on them. A few are listed below.

Bob Larson Ministries
Box 36480
Denver, CO 80236
Ministry dealing with cults.

CARIS
Box 2067
Costa Mesa, CA 92626
Christian apologetics and information on cults and the occult.

Dr. Walter Martin
Christian Research Institute
Box 500
San Juan Capistrano, CA 92693
  Information on cults and the occult.

Eric Pement
Cornerstone Religious Research
4704 N. Malden
Chicago, IL 60640
  New Age tracts and *Cornerstone* magazine.

Cult Awareness Network
2421 W. Pratt Blvd.
Chicago, IL 60645
(312) 267-7777
  Information on cults and satanism.

Evangelical Ministries to New Religions
Box 10000
Denver, CO 80210
  Ministry to the New Age.

Institute for Contemporary Christianity
Box A
Oakland, NJ 07436
(201) 337-0005
  Cult information.

Spiritual Counterfeits Project
Box 2418
Berkeley, CA 94702
Referral hotline: (415) 540-0300

APPENDIX

Books and Articles

New Age

Groothuis, Douglas. "Confronting the New Age Counterfeit." *Equipping the Saints*. Fall, 1988: 2–8.

———. *Unmasking the New Age*. Downers Grove, Ill.: InterVarsity Press, 1986.

Hoyt, Karen, and J. Isamu Yamamoto, eds. *The New Age Rage*. Old Tappan, N.J.: Fleming H. Revell Co., 1987.

Passantino, Bob and Gretchen. "When Christians Meet New Agers." *Christian Herald*. February, 1988: 51–53.

Reisser, Paul C., Teri K. Reisser, and John Weldon. *New Age Medicine*. Downers Grove, Ill.: InterVarsity Press, 1987.

Watring, Richard. "New Age Training in Business: Mind Control in Upper Management?" *Eternity*. February, 1988: 30–34.

Cults and the Occult

Larson, Bob. *Larson's Book of Cults*. Wheaton, Ill.: Tyndale House Pub., 1982.

Peterson, Brian. "Satanic Crime in America." *Charisma and Christian Life*. October, 1988: 34.

Raschke, Carl. "A Growing Darkness: Satanism in America." *Eternity*. October, 1988: 29, 30.

SOURCE NOTES

Introduction

1. Katherine Kam, "In the Name of Satan," *Burrel's* (November 8, 1987), C9.
2. C. S. Lewis, *The Screwtape Letters* (New York: Macmillan Co., 1948), 9.

Chapter 1

1. Bob Batz, Jr., "Tuning Into Samuel," *Marietta Daily Journal* (March 6, 1988), 2E.
2. Doug Underwood, "Harmonic Celebrants," *Seattle Times* (August 17, 1987), B5.
3. Philip Hilts, "Planets Won't Attend Astronomical Celebration," *Washington Post* (July 16, 1987), B3.

4. Ibid.
5. Amy Malick, "New Dollars Ride Crest of New Age," *Durango Herald* (October 12, 1987), A11.
6. "Crystal Consciousness," *Anchorage Times* (October 17, 1987), B2.
7. Gary Yandel, "The Different Facets of the Crystal Craze," *Atlanta Journal* (October 16, 1987).
8. Dolfyn, *Crystal Wisdom* (Novato, Calif.: Earthspirit, Inc., 1985), 7.
9. Bill Dietrich, *Seattle Times* (January 18, 1987), B7.
10. "The Doctrine of Self," *Fundamentalist Journal* (February, 1988), 36.
11. Malick, *Durango Herald*, A11
12. Ibid.
13. Jeffrey Leib, "Bending the New Age to Business," *Denver Post* (November 16, 1987), C11.
14. Richard Watring, "New Age Training in Business: Mind Control in Upper Management?" *Eternity* (February, 1988), 31.
15. Kathleen Hayes, "New Age Music Can Be Hazardous to Your Health," *The NRI Trumpet* (January, 1988), 2.
16. Paul C. Reisser, Teri K. Reisser, John Weldon, *New Age Medicine* (Downers Grove, Ill.: InterVarsity Press, 1987), 64, 65.
17. Reisser, *New Age Medicine*, 135–142; Douglas R. Groothuis, *Unmasking the New Age* (Downers Grove, Ill.: InterVarsity Press, 1986), 68.
18. Karen C. Hoyt, "Personal Growth: Finding or Losing the Self," *The New Age Rage*, ed. Karen Hoyt and J. Isamu Yamamoto (Old Tappan, N.J.: Fleming H. Revell Co., 1987), 179.
19. Douglas Groothuis, "New Age or Ancient Error," *Moody Monthly* (February, 1985), 20.
20. Jessica Lipnack and Jeffrey Stamps, *Networking Book:*

People Connecting With People (New York: Doubleday & Co., 1982).

21. Marilyn Ferguson, *The Aquarian Conspiracy: Personal and Social Transformation in the 1980s* (Los Angeles: Jeremy P. Tarcher, 1981).

Chapter 2

1. Saint Germain, *Keepers of the Flame* (Livingston, Mont.: Summit Lighthouse, 1975), 1–35.
2. "What Is Yoga?" *Boy's Magazine* (December, 1984), 5.
3. Maharishi Mahesh Yogi, *On the Bhagavad-Gita* (New York: Penguin Books, 1969), 224.
4. Gary Bonnelle, "The Ascension Class Series, ' *The Ascension Principle* (Summer, 1988), 7.
5. Jack Purcell, "An Interview With Lazaris," *New Age News* (April, 1988), 4.
6. Mary Platt, "Ascension With Father Andre," *New Age News* (May, 1988), 12.

Chapter 3

1. Lea Schultz, "Ascension Is the Promise," *New Age News* (May, 1988), 9.
2. Gary Bonnelle, "Ascension, Just the Beginning," *New Age News* (May, 1988), 10.
3. Ibid.
4. Gary Bonnelle, "The Ascension Class Series," *The Ascension Principle* (Spring-Summer, 1988), 7.
5. Andris Priede, "Ascension: The Next Journey," *New Age News* (May, 1988), 11.
6. Mary Pratt, "Ascension With Father Andre," *New Age News* (May, 1988), 12.

7. Carrie Dolan, "Try a Brain Tuneup," *Wall Street Journal* (October 21, 1987), 1.
8. Ibid.

Chapter 4

1. Darlyne Pettiniccho, gang consultant lecturer at Center for the Administration of Justice, University of Southern California (January 23, 1985).
2. Denise Linke, "Satanists Focus on Bored, Curious Teens," *The Voice of Bensenville/Wood Dale* (February 17, 1988), section 2, 28.
3. Charlotte Graham, "Satan at Work," *Clarion Ledger* (April 9, 1988), C1.
4. *Devil Worship: Exposing Satan's Underground*, aired October 25, 1988.
5. Texe Marrs, *Dark Secrets of the New Age* (Westchester, Ill.: Crossway Books, 1988), 73.
6. Derk K. Roelofsma, "Battling Satanism," *Insight* (January 11, 1988), 50.
7. *Devil Worship*.
8. Marvin Halversan and Arthur Cohen, eds. "Demons, Demonic, and the Devil," *A Handbook of Christian Theology* (Cleveland: World Publishing, 1965), 76.
9. Robert J. Barry, "Satanism," *National Law Enforcement Magazine* (February, 1987), 40.
10. Richard Cavendish, *The Black Arts* (New York: Putnam & Sons, 1967), 48.
11. Ibid., 247.
12. Melissa Berg, "Fascination With Occult Spans Centuries," *Kansas City Times* (March 26, 1988), A19.
13. "A Parent's Primer on Satanism," *Woman's Day* (November 22, 1988), 150.
14. "Adolescents Susceptible to Satan," *Rocky Mountain News* (March 16, 1987), E5.

15. Roelofsma, "Battling Satanism."
16. Brian Peterson, "Satanic Crime in America," *Charisma and Christian Life* (October, 1988), 34.
17. Carl Raschke, "A Growing Darkness: Satanism in America," *Eternity* (October, 1988), 29.
18. Peterson, "Satanic Crime," 34.

Chapter 5

1. Lisa Ryckman, "Self-Styled Satanism a Growing Cult Among Teens," *Marietta Daily Journal* (February 14, 1988), A6.
2. Kathy Scruggs, "Teens Interested in Occult," *Atlanta Journal* (February 8, 1988), A9.
3. *The Hot 200* (Cardiff, Calif.: New Song Publishing, 1988), 34, 15.
4. Burton H. Wolfe, "The Church That Worships Satan," *Knight Magazine* (September, 1968), 6:30.
5. Anton S. LaVey, *The Satanic Bible* (New York: Avon Books, 1969), 21.
6. Ibid., 57.
7. Ibid., 39.
8. Anton S. LaVey, *The Satanic Rituals* (New York: Avon Books, 1972), 20.
9. Brian Vachon, "Witches Are Rising," *Look* (August 24, 1971), 40.

Chapter 6

1. Sharon Rufus, "Who Are the Witches?" *Fate* (August, 1986), 59.
2. "Witches in U.S. Military Forces," *Daily Oklahoman* (November 27, 1987), 19.

SOURCE NOTES

3. John Kerr, *The Mystery and Magic of the Occult* (Philadelphia: Fortress Press, 1971), 79.

4. Anne Burris, "Bewitching Couple," *Herald* (November 7, 1987), 7.

5. Todd Ackerman, "Wicca," *National Catholic Register* (March 9, 1986), 1.

6. Sybil Leek, *The Complete Art of Witchcraft* (New York: World Publishing, 1971), 11.

7. Ackerman, "Wicca," 10.

8. Anne Burris, "Bewitching Couple Comes Out of the Broom Closet," *Syracuse Herald* (July 31, 1983), L1.

9. Warren Fiske, "Inmate Can Practice Witchcraft," *Virginia-Pilot* (September 6, 1986), 47.

10. "Halloween," *Encyclopedia Britannica*, 11th ed., vol. 12 (Cambridge: Cambridge University Press, 1910), 857, 858.

11. *World Book Encyclopedia* (Chicago, Ill.: Field Enterprises Educational Corp., 1959), 3245, 3246.

12. James Napier, *Folklore* (Philadelphia: Richard West Publishing, 1978), 11.

13. Richard W. DeHaan, *Satan, Satanism, and Witchcraft* (Grand Rapids, Mich.: Zondervan Pub. House, 1972), 98.

14. Pearle Epstein, *The Way of Witches* (Garden City, N.Y.: Doubleday & Co., 1972), 66.

15. Ibid., 98.

16. Sybil Leek, *Complete Art*, 76.

17. Ackerman, "Wicca," 1.

18. Joseph Bayly, *What About Horoscopes?* (Elgin, Ill.: David C. Cook Pub. Co., 1970), 22.

19. V. Raymond Edman, "Divine or Devilish," *Christian Herald* (May, 1964), 16.

Chapter 7

1. William D. Eisenhower, "Your Devil Is Too Small," *Christianity Today* (July 15, 1988), 24, 25.

2. Charles Hodge, *Systematic Theology*, vol. 1 (Grand Rapids, Mich.: Eerdmans, 1982), 644, 646, 647.
3. *Atlanta Journal* (October, 1972).
4. Arthur Drago and Kathy Jumper, "Dungeons and Dragons," *Mobile Press Register* (May 4, 1986), D3.
5. Jerry Johnston, *Why Suicide* (Nashville, Tenn.: Thomas Nelson/Oliver-Nelson, 1987), 87.

Chapter 8

1. Bob and Gretchen Passantino, "When Christians Meet New Agers," *Christian Herald* (February, 1988), 51.
2. Stan Baldwin, *Games Satan Plays* (Wheaton, Ill.: Victor Books, 1971), 27.
3. James A. Pike and Diane Kennedy, *The Other Side* (New York: Doubleday & Co., 1968), 115.
4. Victor H. Ernest, *I Talked With Spirits* (Wheaton, Ill.: Tyndale House Pub., 1971), 48.
5. David Marlow, "Psychic Quackery," *People* (April /, 1988), 149.
6. Ruth Montgomery, *A Gift of Prophecy* (New York: Bantam Books, 1966), 17.
7. *The Herald News* (January 27, 1968), 7.
8. John D. Davis, "Familiar Spirit," *Davis Dictionary of the Bible* (Westwood, N.J.: Fleming H. Revell Co., 1924), 228.
9. Karen Hoyt, "Personal Growth: Finding or Losing the Self," *The New Age Rage*, ed. Karen Hoyt and J. Isamu Yamamoto (Old Tappan, N.J.: Fleming H. Revell Co., 1987), 183.

Chapter 9

1. Joyce Wadler, "The President's Astrologers," *People* (May 23, 1988), 111.

SOURCE NOTES

2. Suzanne M. Schafer, "Regan Portrays Reagan," *Marietta Daily Journal* (May 9, 1988), 1.
3. J. A. Sargent, "Astrology's Rising Star," *Christianity Today* (February 4, 1983), 37.
4. Daniel Cohen, *Myths of the Space Age* (New York: Dodd, Mead & Co., 1967).
5. Louis MacNeice, *Astrology* (Garden City, N.Y.: Doubleday & Co., 1964), 113.
6. Michael Gauquelin, *The Cosmic Clocks* (New York: Avon Books, 1969), 84.
7. Rupert Gleadow, *The Origin of the Zodiac* (New York: Atheneum Press, 1969), 55.
8. John Weldon and Clifford Wilson, *Occult Shock* (San Diego: Masters Books, 1983), 111.
9. Karen C. Hoyt, "Introduction," *The New Age Rage*, ed. Karen Hoyt and J. Isamu Yamamoto (Old Tappan, N.J.: Fleming H. Revell Co., 1987), 11.
10. MacNeice, *Astrology*.
11. Richard Hammar, *The Pentecostal Evangel* (December 15, 1985), 1.
12. Maxwell Maltz, *Psycho-Cybernetics* (New York: Prentice-Hall, 1960), ix.
13. William Smith, "Magi," *Smith's Bible Dictionary* (Westwood, N.J.: Fleming H. Revell Co., n.d.), 364.
14. F. King, *The Cosmic Influence* (Garden City, N.Y.: Doubleday & Co., 1976), 41.
15. Gauquelin, *Cosmic Clocks*, 85, 86.
16. Steve Cooper, "Don't Put Any Faith in It," *San Bernardino Sun* (July 20, 1986), F12.

Chapter 10

1. Robert S. Ellwood, *Religious and Spiritual Groups in Modern America* (Englewood Cliffs, N.J.: Prentice-Hall, Inc., 1973), 304.

2. Bob Larson, *Larson's Book of Cults* (Wheaton, Ill.: Tyndale House Pub., 1982), 43.
3. William J. Petersen, *Those Curious New Cults in the Eighties* (New Canaan, Conn.: Keats Pub., 1982), 125, 127.

Chapter 11

1. Kenneth L. Woodward, "The Exorcism Frenzy," *Newsweek* (February 11, 1974), 61.
2. Ibid.

Chapter 12

1. Douglas Groothuis, "Confronting the New Age Counterfeit," *Equipping the Saints* (Fall, 1988), 4.
2. Scott McMurray, "Real Witches Today Don't Stew Newts, Not in Wisconsin," *Wall Street Journal*, eastern edition (October 31, 1988), 1.
3. Brian Peterson, "Satanic Crime in America," *Charisma and Christian Life* (October, 1988), 34.
4. William J. Petersen, *Those Curious New Cults in the Eighties* (New Canaan, Conn.: Keats Pub., 1982), 165.
5. Carroll Stoner and Jo Anne Parke, *All God's Children* (New York: Penguin Books, 1977), 326.